Living in the Middle Ages

Dianne Zarlengo, *Book Editor*

Bruce Glassman, *Vice President*
Bonnie Szumski, *Publisher*
Helen Cothran, *Managing Editor*

San Diego • Detroit • New York • San Francisco • Cleveland
New Haven, Conn. • Waterville, Maine • London • Munich

For more information, contact
Greenhaven Press
27500 Drake Rd.
Farmington Hills, MI 48331-3535
Or you can visit our Internet site at http://www.gale.com

Cover credit: © Réunion des Musées Nationaux/Art Resource, NY
Dover Publications, 39
North Wind Picture Archives, 70, 79, 97

LIBRARY OF CONGRESS CATALOGING-IN-PUBLICATION DATA

Living in the Middle Ages / Dianne Zarlengo, book editor.
p. cm. — (Exploring cultural history)
Includes bibliographical references and index.
ISBN 0-7377-2092-1 (lib. : alk. paper) — ISBN 0-7377-2093-X (pbk. : alk. paper)
1. Europe—Social life and customs. 2. Social history—Medieval, 500–1500.
3. Civilization, medieval. 4. Middle Ages. I. Zarlengo, Dianne. II. Series.
GT120.L585 2004
306'.094'0902—dc22 2003049386

Printed in the United States of America

Contents

Chapter 2: Community and Work

Chapter 3: Trials and Tribulations

Foreword

Too often, history books and teachers place an overemphasis on events and dates. Students learn that key births, battles, revolutions, coronations, and assassinations occurred in certain years. But when many centuries separate these happenings from the modern world, they can seem distant, disconnected, even irrelevant.

The reality is that today's society is *not* disconnected from the societies that preceded it. In fact, modern culture is a sort of melting pot of various aspects of life in past cultures. Over the course of centuries and millennia, one culture passed on some of its traditions, in the form of customs, habits, ideas, and beliefs, to another, which modified and built on them to fit its own needs. That culture then passed on its own version of the traditions to later cultures, including today's. Pieces of everyday life in past cultures survive in our own lives, therefore. And it is often these morsels of tradition, these survivals of tried and true past experience, that people most cherish, take comfort in, and look to for guidance. As the great English scholar and archaeologist Sir Leonard Woolley put it, "We cannot divorce ourselves from our past. We are always conscious of precedents . . . and we let experience shape our views and actions."

Thus, for example, Americans and the inhabitants of a number of other modern nations can pride themselves on living by the rule of law, educating their children in formal schools, expressing themselves in literature and art, and following the moral precepts of various religions and philosophies. Yet modern society did not invent the laws, schools, literature, art, religions, and philosophies that pervade it; rather, it inherited these things from previous cultures. "Time, the great destroyer, is also the great preserver," the late, noted thinker Herbert J. Muller once observed. "It has preserved . . . the immense accumulation of products, skills, styles, customs, institutions, and ideas that make the man on the American street indebted to all the peoples of history, including some who never saw a street." In this way, ancient Mesopotamia gave the world its first cities and literature; ancient Egypt, large-scale architecture; ancient Israel, the formative concepts of Judaism,

Christianity, and Islam; ancient Greece, democracy, the theater, Olympic sports, and magnificent ceramics; ancient China, gunpowder and exotic fabrics; ancient Rome and medieval England, their pioneering legal systems; Renaissance Italy, great painting and sculpture; Elizabethan England, the birth of modern drama; and colonial America, the formative environments of the founders of the United States, the most powerful and prosperous nation in world history. Only by looking back on those peoples and how they lived can modern society understand its roots.

Not all the products of cultural history have been so constructive, however. Most ancient Greeks severely restricted the civil rights and daily lives of women, for instance; the Romans kept and abused large numbers of slaves, as did many Americans in the years preceding the Civil War; and Nazi Germany and the Soviet Union curbed or suppressed freedom of speech, assembly, and religion. Examining these negative aspects of life in various past cultures helps to expose the origins of many of the social problems that exist today; it also reminds us of the ever-present potential for people to make mistakes and pursue misguided or destructive social and economic policies.

The books in the Greenhaven Press Exploring Cultural History series provide readers with the major highlights of life in human cultures from ancient times to the present. The family, home life, food and drink, women's duties and rights, childhood and education, arts and leisure, literacy and literature, roads and means of communications, slavery, religious beliefs, and more are examined in essays grouped by theme. The essays in each volume have been chosen for their readability and edited to manageable lengths. Many are primary sources. These original voices from a past culture echo through the corridors of time and give the volume a strong feeling of immediacy and authenticity. The other essays are by historians and other modern scholars who specialize in the culture in question. An annotated table of contents, chronology, and extensive bibliography broken down by theme add clarity and context. Thus, each volume in the Greenhaven Press Exploring Cultural History series opens a unique window through which readers can gaze into a distant time and place and eavesdrop on life in a long vanished culture.

Introduction: Medieval Life—the Impact of Social Status on Everyday Living

Social status determined the quality of life in the Middle Ages. The class status into which a person was born determined the lifestyle, the type of marriage, and even the kind of burial one would receive. The poorest in society worked from sunrise to sunset every day, the peasants trying to keep from starving and striving to pay monies to the lord. The shopkeepers, craftspeople, and laborers worked long hours struggling to attain a better lifestyle. The wealthy and powerful fought wars, managed vast landholdings, and enjoyed their leisure time.

Feudalism and Manorialism

Medieval social classes had their roots in feudalism and manorialism, social systems that sprang up after the fall of the Roman Empire. The beginning of the Middle Ages (around A.D. 500) was a chaotic time. The Roman Empire with its centralized government had fallen, thereby allowing invaders and marauders to prey on weaker societies. Throughout Europe, people fled from the cities to the countryside, escaping the invading forces and finding temporary refuge until the invading armies decimated their settlements. Barbaric tribes such as the Huns (from central Asia), the Franks, Goths, and Burgundians (all Germanic), the Vikings, the Magyars (the Hungarians), and the Muslims (from North Africa and the Middle East) waged war continually in order to conquer and acquire more territories. By the eighth and ninth centuries, centralized states such as the Carolingian Empire (which controlled lands in what are now France, Germany, England, Austria, the Netherlands, and northern Italy) could not effectively defend their people against the invasions of the Vikings, Magyars, and Muslims. Not only did the weak central governments have problems defending their people against foreign invaders, they also had trouble protecting their people from civil wars between nobles within their own territories. In addition, the governments could not control or suppress bandits or highwaymen who preyed on travelers and on rural settlements. During these times great turbulence and insecurity existed, and the people, lacking faith in the central government, turned to the local lord for protection. Around A.D. 911 a new social order—feudalism—began to emerge in Europe.

Feudalism, which had been actively practiced in China for centuries prior to its arrival in Europe, was a system based on mutual obligations. In theory, the head of the feudal system was the king; in actuality, the king had authority only over his personal lands, while his vassals had authority over the rest of the land. A vassal was a lord who was granted land (known as a fief) and who had specific obligations, such as military service, to render in exchange for his land. The vassal then granted fiefs to knights or lords, who became his vassals or subvassals. The subvassals owed military protection to the vassal who had granted them their fief. An example of this arrangement might look as follows: King grants land (fief) to nobleman (vassal) in exchange for nobleman's military protection. Nobleman does not have an army, so he in turn grants land to knight (subvassal) who renders military services to nobleman and ultimately to king. The feudal system was primarily concerned with power, land, and military protection. During the time when feudalism flourished, military protection was an absolute necessity. The feudal relationship only concerned the wealthy classes; the peasants, who made up most of the population of medieval Europe, were not part of the feudal network.

The system of relationships between peasants and their lords was manorialism. The manorial system was the most basic and widespread economic system in much of Europe until the Late Middle Ages. Since Europe's economy was chiefly based on agriculture, the majority of the population either worked or managed the land. The manor was an estate held by a lord and made up of the lord's demesne (the lord's lands held by peasants). Estates varied in size from five hundred acres to five thousand acres. The estate was a self-contained village governed by the lord and consisting of a mill, a forge, a church, a barnyard, a baking house, a weaving house, and a wash house. The lord depended on his estate to provide his household with cheese, grain, and meat. The peasants living on the estate worked the lord's land in exchange for land of their own and for protection. In theory, the manor system was one of mutual obligations: The lord gave land and protection to the peasant, and the peasant gave his labor and produce to the lord. In actuality, the balance of power favored the lord, and the peasant endured a life of hardship.

From the beginning of the Middle Ages until the close of the period, the peasant's life was difficult at best. Even though the peasants provided the labor that enabled the society to survive, they were often scorned by the wealthier classes. The peasants had to sustain the lord's lifestyle while trying to produce enough food to feed their own families. The lord always received his produce from the peasants regardless of whether there was enough produce left over to sustain the peasants' households. In the cold winter months, more often than not, peasants had to rely on tree bark and plant roots to stave off hunger and death until the spring and summer harvests. Many did not prevail; however, the lord's household rarely lost family members to starvation. The English poet William Langland (circa 1330 to circa 1400) describes the harsh realities of life for the peasant in his famous allegorical poem, *Piers Plowman*:

> The neediest are our neighbors, if we just notice them:
> prisoners in holes and poor folk in huts,
> overburdened by children and oppressive landlords.
> What they save from their spinning they spend on house-rent,
> on milk and oatmeal to make porridge
> to fill their children when they cry for food.
> They themselves suffer the sting of hunger
> and of winter misery, rising at night
> to rock the cradle in its cramped corner,
> to card and comb wool, to mend and wash,
> to scrub and wind yarn, to weave rushlights. . . .
> Bread and thin ale are their only share,
> cold meat and fish instead of fine venison;
> on Fridays and fast days a penny's-worth of mussels
> or a few cockles are a feast for such folk.[1]

Peasants: Serfs and Freemen

Peasants made up the greater part of the medieval population. Their class formed the economic backbone for the society. Labor constituted the bulk of the peasants' everyday life. In medieval times, the term *peasant* simply meant the class of people who worked the land in order to feed the aristocracy. The peasant class was the lowest rung on the medieval social ladder. Within the general peasant class, two subclasses of peasants existed: serfs and freemen. Each subclass had different rights and obligations, and at times the two classes merged into each other. The serf's lack of freedom was the most notable difference between the two groups.

Serfdom had two origins. Many serfs were descendants of slaves of the Roman Empire, while others were formerly freemen who had descended into serfdom due to poverty or the need for protection from a lord. Although serfs were not slaves in the sense that they could not be bought or sold, they belonged to the land and they passed on to another generation of lordship as did the land. Serfs required a specific act of liberation to gain or regain a state of personal freedom. Therefore, the major features of serfdom were lack of freedom and complete dependence on the lord. Serfs could not leave the land or marry without the lord's permission. They owed obligations to the lord such as tilling his fields and maintaining the upkeep of the manor. They performed a multitude of required tasks, including laundering, milling, repairing roads, tending livestock, and brewing beer. Serfs lived a life of drudgery and constant work. After performing their required duties for the lord, they cultivated a small parcel of land which was theirs as long as the lord deemed it to be.

In contrast, freemen who lived on the manor could leave the manor freely. Most freemen sought the lord's protection, thus they leased parcels of land from the lord. In the Early Middle Ages, the rent from the leased land was paid to the lord in services and in crop yields. As the Middle Ages progressed, it became more common for the rent to be paid by money. Even though the freeman owed the lord services such as repairing the manor's roads and fences, his duties were not as numerous as the serf's, and he could leave the land or marry whomever he pleased without first obtaining the lord's permission. Sometimes freemen were able to purchase their leased parcel of land, thus elevating their financial status.

Theoretically, the freeman was in a better position than the serf because he was able to quit the land and leave of his own accord. However, in actuality, the line that separated serf from freeman was not always clear-cut. The freeman was expected to pay taxes and services to the lord, and in doing so, many freemen found themselves incurring more and more debt until their free status slipped into a secondary status of serfdom. Many freemen could never leave the manor due to the fact that they owed too much money to the lord and were therefore bound to the manor as were the serfs.

In addition to the steep fees charged for use of the land, both serfs and freemen had to pay the lord for the use of the manor's facilities. The lord required all peasants to perform their daily living tasks such as slaughtering their livestock, churning their butter, and laundering their clothes at the manor's facilities for an exorbitant fee. Any attempt by the peasants to use facilities outside the manor was treated as a crime met with punishment and monetary penalties. A surviving document from the Saint Denis monastery in La Chapelle, France, in the twelfth century describes some of the penalties imposed upon the peasantry:

> If anyone, living between the four crosses, bakes bread elsewhere than in the oven of St. Denis, and this is proved, he shall first pay the charge for baking and then a fine.
>
> If anyone has a damper and habitually bakes his bread below it, the damper shall be broken and he shall pay a fine.
>
> Similarly, if it is proved that someone has ground grain elsewhere than in the saint's mill, he shall pay the right of multure and a fine.
>
> It is laid down that every inhabitant of La Chapelle who shall expose wine to sell shall give the monks one setier per cask.[2]

After a hard day's work, the peasants trudged to their humble homes, which were scattered around the manor. An average peasant's house featured an attached barn housing the family's livestock (mostly chickens and a pig). The ceiling was fashioned from woven straw and thicket, the walls from stone or timber, and the dirt floors were strewn with rushes, straw, or, on special occasions, herbs and wildflowers. In addition to the barn, there were two rooms, one for eating and living, the other for sleeping. Small windows covered by oiled paper (glass was used only in the homes of the very wealthy) brought some light into the abode. The sole source of heat was a central hearth in the living area that burned all day, and the house was invariably smoky since there was no chimney or ventilation. Cooking was done over the burning hearth, and the meals consisted mostly of a thick stew or soup of root vegetables, called pottage, and a piece of dark bread. Salted meats and fish were an occasional luxury. Because they could not afford to purchase the necessary alimentation for a balanced diet, most peasants were severely malnourished.

Peasant homes were sparsely furnished with only a long table, a wood bench, a wood trunk, and one or two straw mattresses. Inside bathrooms did not exist; the peasants used a communal well to relieve themselves. Bathing was not engaged in often, and when it was, the bathtub was a barrel filled with heated water, which the entire family used. As a result of the lack of hygiene and sanitation, houses and bodies had lice and fleas, and rats were common.

Peasants, for the most part, accepted their lot in life. Serfs believed their class status was inherited from their ancestors. The freeman viewed his hardships as part of his fate. Through all the toiling and sweat, the concept of original sin intertwined itself around the peasant's life, as pointed out by historian Hans-Werner Goetz: "Of course, the attitude toward work was ambivalent. On the one hand, work was considered a curse, the consequence of original sin; on the other hand, it was also understood as penance during life on earth, and as such it was pleasing to God."[3]

Even though the burdened peasant class largely accepted their harsh life as a way to cleanse their souls and help pave the way to eternal salvation, peasants revolted occasionally. During the period spanning the ninth to thirteenth centuries, laborers sporadically attempted to better their condition in life by refusing to work or to pay the lord. These small disturbances were disorganized, poorly supported, and easily quashed by the lord. Afterward, the peasants went back to the monotony of a life of labor. However, by the fourteenth century, peasant revolts were becoming commonplace all over Europe due to rising rents and taxes, inflation, poor harvests, famine, and the plague. Revolts occurred in France, England, Germany, Spain, Italy, and Belgium. These revolts were larger and better organized than previous uprisings.

One of the most infamous revolts of the Middle Ages was the Peasants' Revolt in 1381. Led by freeman Wat Tyler, the uprising was directed against poll taxation imposed on the population to pay for the war with France (a poll tax, or head tax, takes the same amount of money from everyone regardless of their means, thus laying a heavier burden on the poor). Successful in the beginning but ultimately crushed by the ruling class, Tyler was captured and executed; however, the revolt of 1381, as well as other uprisings in France and Italy, led to changes throughout Europe. According to authors Frances and Joseph Gies:

> All the risings were suppressed, naturally, by the united upper class—monarchy, nobility, upper clergy, wealthy townsmen—but all nevertheless left their mark. In England the poll tax was abandoned. . . . Everywhere, the process by which serfdom was withering was accelerated. . . .Quietly and unobtrusively, an era in social relations was closing.[4]

The Nobility

In sharp contrast to the peasantry, those born into the noble class inherited a life of power and luxury. Nobles were the medieval ruling class, and they claimed their right to rule based on their high birth. Their innate qualities, it was believed, were inherited from a family line of nobles. The economic power of the nobles rested in their control of the land and in their capacity to exploit the majority of the population (the freemen and the serfs). Their social power stemmed from their ability to support their lifestyle, thus maintaining the respect of the masses.

To a modern observer, the lifestyle of the nobility was a mixture of luxury and simplicity. The wealthy lived in stone castles or large homes that had numerous rooms, including the great hall, the public room where residents and visitors ate, conversed, and slept. The residences were sparsely furnished with only wood beds, chests, trunks, tapestries (large wall hangings used for decoration and to keep out drafts), several ornate wooden chairs, and a long dining table. Furniture was viewed as a practical necessity, and because nobles often had more than one castle, furniture had to be portable so that it could travel with them from castle to castle. The aristocratic residence had just a few more pieces of furniture than the peasant household, but the quality of furniture was

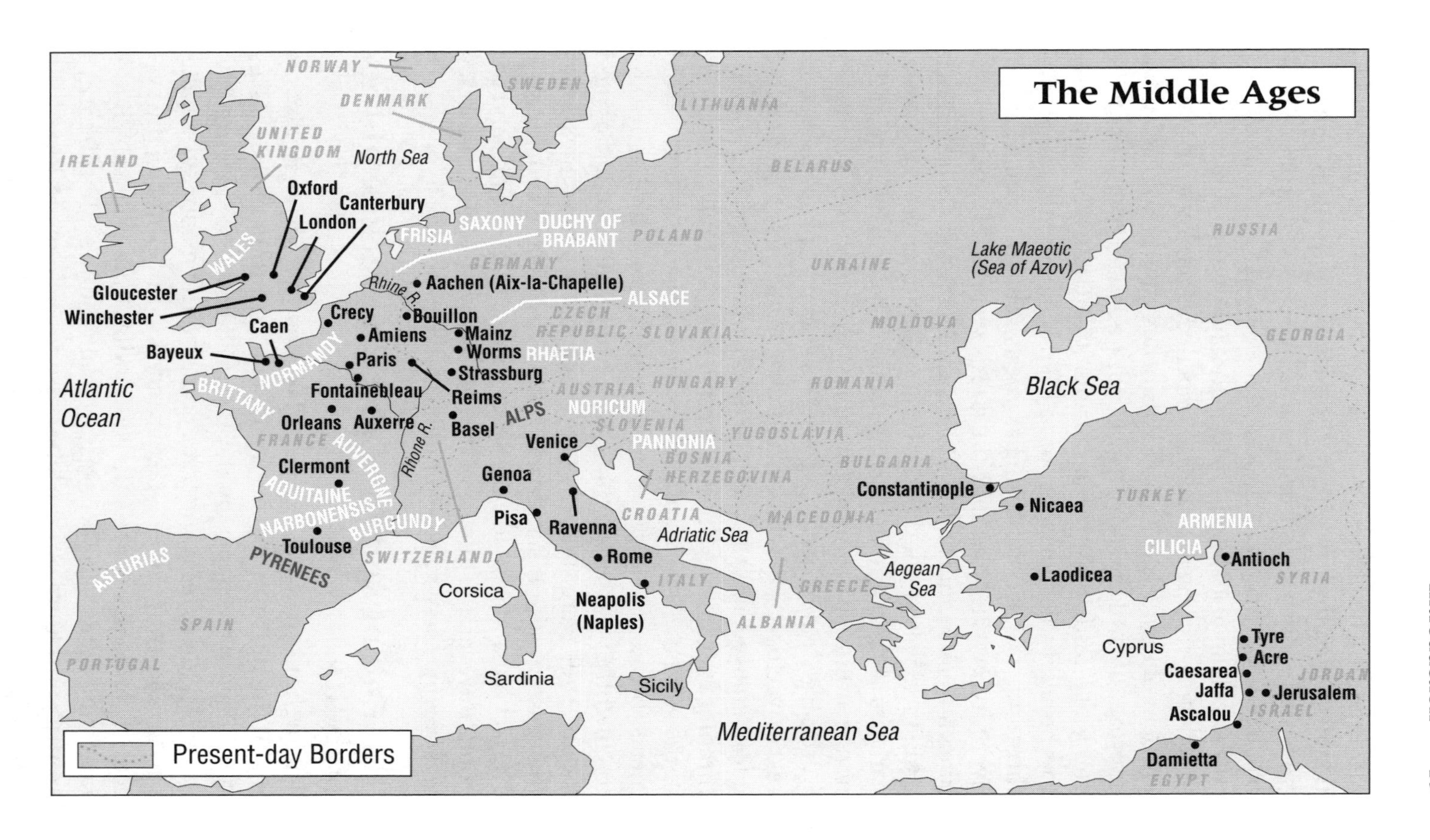

The Middle Ages
Present-day Borders
Atlantic Ocean
North Sea
Black Sea
Lake Maeotic (Sea of Azov)
Aegean Sea
Adriatic Sea
Mediterranean Sea
IRELAND
UNITED KINGDOM
NORWAY
DENMARK
SWEDEN
LITHUANIA
BELARUS
RUSSIA
POLAND
UKRAINE
MOLDOVA
GEORGIA
GERMANY
CZECH REPUBLIC
SLOVAKIA
HUNGARY
ROMANIA
AUSTRIA
SLOVENIA
BOSNIA HERZEGOVINA
CROATIA
YUGOSLAVIA
BULGARIA
MACEDONIA
ALBANIA
GREECE
TURKEY
SYRIA
JORDAN
ISRAEL
EGYPT
ITALY
SWITZERLAND
FRANCE
SPAIN
PORTUGAL
WALES
BRITTANY
NORMANDY
AUVERGNE
AQUITAINE
NARBONENSIS
BURGUNDY
PYRENEES
ASTURIAS
FRISIA
SAXONY
DUCHY OF BRABANT
ALSACE
RHAETIA
NORICUM
PANNONIA
ALPS
ARMENIA
CILICIA
Oxford
Canterbury
London
Gloucester
Winchester
Caen
Bayeux
Crecy
Amiens
Paris
Fontainebleau
Orleans
Auxerre
Clermont
Toulouse
Aachen (Aix-la-Chapelle)
Bouillon
Mainz
Worms
Strassburg
Reims
Basel
Rhine R.
Rhone R.
Venice
Genoa
Pisa
Ravenna
Rome
Neapolis (Naples)
Corsica
Sardinia
Sicily
Constantinople
Nicaea
Laodicea
Antioch
Cyprus
Tyre
Acre
Caesarea
Jaffa
Jerusalem
Ascalou
Damietta

far superior. The affluent could afford to have well-made items that displayed their wealth in the richness of the items' decoration, with lavishly embroidered fabrics, carved and ornately painted woodwork, and enameled metalwork.

The nobility usually left the day-to-day running of their estates to stewards, freeing themselves for periodic military duty and enjoyment of their leisure hours. Aristocrats entertained each other continually and lavishly. It was not unusual for visitors to be guests at a castle for three to four months. These well-to-do visitors brought their servants, their friends, and their family; thus the number of people staying as guests at a castle could be well over fifty. During their stay, the guests were entertained several times a week by minstrels, jugglers, magicians, and dancers. Their main meal was at noon in the great hall and consisted of several varieties of meat and fish, fruits (oranges being a delicacy in the northern European countries), some vegetables (root vegetables were rarely eaten because they were seen as peasants' food), cakes sweetened with honey, and wine. After the noon meal, the guests enjoyed leisure time: The men whiled away their time by hunting and gaming, the women by embroidering and strolling in the gardens. The evening hours provided a light supper (cold meats, bread, and cheese), chess games, songs, and dances by torchlight. Even though the nobles enjoyed a life of luxury and leisure, they were still subject to some of the same hardships as the peasants (the Black Death, floods, fires, wars, and famine). The fact is that the Middle Ages was a struggle for the rich and the poor; however, the quality of day-to-day living of the aristocracy was beyond the wildest aspirations of the peasantry.

The End of Serfdom and the Decline of the Nobility

Throughout the Middle Ages, class distinctions were always maintained. However, the social configuration of the classes slowly began to change by the Late Middle Ages. Most notably, as the Middle Ages waned, serfdom and the manor system began to fade away. Several factors aided in undermining the system of serfdom: Europe's transformation from primarily agrarian to mostly urban societies beginning in the late thirteenth century; the demand for labor due to the decimation of life caused by the Black Death in the fourteenth century; the numerous peasant revolts of the fourteenth century; and the serfs' increasing dissatisfaction with their lot in life. By the end of the Middle Ages, serfdom in western Europe no longer existed; however, it was still thriving in eastern Europe, where it continued to do so until the late nineteenth century (especially in Russia).

The emergence of cities in the thirteenth century contributed to the decline of serfdom. In French cities, a general movement for emancipation eventually made serfs a minority of the peasant population. In the Italian city-states, governments eliminated personal servitude as a way to dilute the power of the aristocracy and to increase the number of taxpayers. To increase their city's population, many towns and cities throughout western Europe granted privileges to their inhabitants. One such privilege was freedom to serfs; if a former serf lived in a city for a year and a day, he or she was free from obligations toward the lord of the land to which he or she had been tied. An 1188 document written by King Philip Augustus of France, granted such rights to the community of Pontoise: "All who dwell in the parishes of Pontoise and St. Martin shall by perpetual right be free and immune from every unjust tallage, from unjustified arrest, from unfair use of the right to purchase their goods, and from all unreasonable exactions."[5]

Hence, many serfs fled the manor to find freedom and a better life in the cities throughout western Europe. These former serfs opened blacksmith shops, bakeries, and mills and engaged in a number of trades such as ale making, mining, and tailoring. For the first time in their lives, they were able to enjoy the fruits of their labor.

While the state of serfdom began to dissipate, the demarcation between nobility and knights also began to erode due to the Crusades. Prior to the twelfth century, knights were above the peasantry, but because of their poor and humble origins, they were far below the nobility on the social ladder. When the church entered into the Crusades in the late eleventh century, the social status of knights grew. The distinct line that had divided knights and nobility now became blurred as knights began to own their own lands, thus enabling the two classes to merge and create one enlarged aristocracy. Although knights were able to amass wealth due to land ownership, most only had enough land to support their families. Due to the rigors of knighthood, few children of knights followed in their fathers' footsteps. Therefore, the knights' family lines were short and their wealth only endured a lifetime.

Another factor that advanced the decline of the landed aristocracy was the death rate among the class. A medieval person had a life expectancy of around thirty-five years if he or she survived childhood. Childhood diseases, contaminated water, and unsanitary conditions meant that many children never reached adulthood. During the thirteenth century, according to historian Jeffrey Singman, "about one child in five died the first year, one in four by age five, and only two-thirds lived to the age of twenty."[6] It was common for medieval families to be small based on the fact that death was ubiquitous. Many nobles suffered a low birthrate (due to infertility) or a high infant mortality rate (due to unclean conditions, diseases, and limited medical knowledge).

The death rate was also high among the male members of the nobility owing to the constant state of war during most of the Middle Ages. Thousands of men were killed in the Hundred Years' War (1337–1453) between England and France. Since the men fighting the wars were from the nobility, many noble households lost husbands, sons, and brothers. The social and economic ramifications of this loss were that there were no sons to inherit the property; if there were no daughters, then the family line was terminated.

The beginning of the twelfth century found a medieval world more politically and religiously stable, thus allowing the shift from an agrarian to urban society to take place. This change made travel safer, thus increasing commerce and trade. As merchants moved more freely, markets increased and money began to be used on a wide scale. An increase in trade and prosperity stimulated the growth of new towns and breathed life into the existing ones.

City Life Among the Classes

The growth of cities created a new social order and led to the development of new social classes. Landowners became businesspeople, former serfs and freemen became shop owners, women entered the workforce, and a burgeoning middle class emerged. The city's upper class consisted of burghers (wealthy merchants), masters of the various labor guilds, and urban landowners. The burghers, a new class of people, lived a pampered life that included fine clothes, elegant parties, and much leisure time.

The middle class was composed of lawyers, doctors, merchants, bankers, and skilled craftsmen, and they were, in most parts of Europe, the leading citizens of a town. Many of the upper-middle-class citizens held city offices and were influential in establishing and modifying the laws in their towns. The lower middle class was made up of artisans, small businesspeople such as shopkeepers and innkeepers, and manufacturers. Many of the lower middle class, including women, came from former peasant lives and enjoyed financial stability and opportunity in the cities and towns. Middle-class women were able to open and run their own businesses (*femmes soles*) apart from their husbands, something a woman in the countryside could only dream about.

The lower class was reserved for assistants, common laborers, and those who engaged in domestic services for the wealthy. The urban lower classes were despised by the city dwellers just as the peasants were by the nobility. Most of urban society looked down on these people, and they were denied the rights given to other members of the society. As Goetz points out:

> Journeymen (in part), apprentices, shop assistants who had not benefited from any training, day laborers, and domestics in wealthy households, all belonged to the lower civic strata. Lower status was also the lot of those born out of wedlock or who practiced certain occupations considered "dishonorable" (such as executioners, skinnners, or undertakers).
>
> Members of the lower strata possessed no civic rights and did not regularly own property, although they did not have the right to be entirely indigent. Their numbers figured prominently among a city's inhabitants, contributing significantly to the typically urban concentration of population as well as to urban life as a whole. Their share in the population is estimated at approximately forty percent.[7]

There was also a significant population who did not fit into any of the above classes. This group was like a subclass and consisted primarily of beggars and prostitutes. The beggars were especially despised, although socially unavoidable. Many cities and towns attempted to enact laws to stop begging, but these laws were of little effect. Others who lived on the fringes of society were the mentally ill and the lepers who were feared and shunned at all costs.

Medieval cities featured timber-framed, thatch-roofed townhouses that were often three to four stories high. Most traders and craftspeople lived in cramped quarters above their stores or workshops, while the more affluent merchants lived in more spacious quarters featuring several rooms and one servant. The more financially equipped doctors or lawyers lived in large stone homes that featured many rooms and many servants. The wealthy merchants and urban landowners lived in stone palaces decorated on the outside with delicately carved rows of marble columns (in Italy), stone statuary (in France and Germany), and stone vignettes of everyday living (in England). These palaces had elaborate windows in stained glass and housed several dozen servants and attendants. The furnishings were not as spartan as they were in the castles of the countryside. Intricately woven tapestries in bold hues of red, gold, blue, yellow, and green adorned the massive walls of these palaces. Rich fabrics from the Orient covered carved, wooden chairs and chests, while lush velvet coverings beautified the bed chambers. The urban rich lived as lavishly in their palaces as the nobles did in their castles, and the very poor lived as miserably in their cramped and damp quarters as the peasants did in their crude huts. There still existed a large dichotomy between the wealthy and the poor in the medieval world.

The struggle to survive the Middle Ages was a challenge for both the rich and the poor. Even though each class faced natural disasters, wars, bubonic plague, and violence, the day-to-day living of the wealthy made the fight more palatable for them, while the poor found little relief from their daily efforts to stay alive. The distinctions between the classes shifted throughout the Middle Ages. The dawn of the Middle Ages revealed an entirely agrarian society with distinct social classes: the aristocracy, the knights, and the peasantry. By the end of the Middle Ages, the shift from rural to urban society resulted in the eradication of earlier classes (serfs) and the formation of new classes (burghers).

As the Middle Ages merged into the Renaissance, a new social and economic order was set in place. However, the chasm between the rich and the poor and between the powerful and the powerless persisted.

Notes

1. Quoted in Margaret Williams, *Piers the Plowman*. New York: Random House, 1971, pp. 58–59.
2. Quoted in Brian Tierney, ed., *The Middle Ages*. New York: McGraw-Hill, 1999, p. 263.
3. Hans-Werner Goetz, *Life in the Middle Ages: From the Seventh to the Thirteenth Century*. Notre Dame, IN: University of Notre Dame Press, 1993, p. 140.
4. Frances and Joseph Gies, *Marriage and the Family in the Middle Ages*. New York: Harper & Row, 1987, p. 78.
5. Quoted in Peter Rietbergen, *Europe: A Cultural History*. London and New York: Routledge, 1998, p. 133.
6. Jeffrey L. Singman, *Daily Life in Medieval England*. Westport, CT: Greenwood Press, 1999, p. 18.
7. Goetz, *Life in the Middle Ages*, p. 228.

Domestic Life

Chapter Preface

In A.D. 1200 an anonymous advocate of monastic life for women observed, "You [medieval women] say . . . man's vigor is worth much, and I need his help for maintenance and food; and of the companionship of woman and man arises well-being, and a family of fair children that greatly please the parents. . . . You say that a wife has much comfort of her husband when they are well matched, and that each is well pleased with the other." These words suggest that many medieval couples saw marriage as a pleasant and desirable state. Actually, marriage was a primary goal for most medieval people and, unless one was entering into a religious life, a domestic life of matrimony and child rearing was expected.

Among the nobility, arranged marriages were the rule. Most of the upper-class betrothals were based exclusively on financial considerations. Upper-class women married as young as twelve years old, with the average age being fifteen, to men who were well into their thirties.

In criticism of arranged marriages, medieval French preacher Jacques de Virty stated, "One might as well publish the banns of Lord Such-and-Such with the purse of Madame So-and-So, and on the day of the wedding lead to the church not the fiancee but her money or her cow." Sharing the preacher's viewpoint, some nobles defied their families by marrying for love. Canon law enabled couples to marry without familial consent, and young lovers took advantage of this loophole by eloping. Medieval writings indicate that men and women fell in love, married, and had fulfilling relationships despite their economic differences.

Peasants and members of the middle class were freer to choose their own spouses. In selecting a mate, economics did not play as important a role as it did in upper-class marriages. Unlike noblewomen, most middle-class wives earned income outside the house and peasant women labored side by side with their husbands in the fields. The unions between men and women of these classes were based more on compatibility and love than on financial gain. Couples within these two classes tended to marry in their twenties.

Medieval society was male-dominated, and the husband was head of the household. Women and children were seen as the property of the husband. The thirteenth-century Florentine moralist E. Barbaro wrote, "Sole master in his own home, the husband does not disclose all the family secrets to his wife. He trains her to perform her wifely duties . . . with due consideration for the fragility of her body and character." Communal statutes like that of Gello (lawmaker) in Tuscany (1373) authorized men to "punish their children, their younger brothers, and also their wives." Legal laws accorded a father even greater authority and control over his children, who were obliged to treat him with respect and total reverence. Disobedient children were treated harshly by many fathers, and the laws of the period endorsed this conduct.

Even though the law and custom of the Middle Ages gave dominion and control of the household to the husband, many medieval families had loving and nurturing unions and spent time together enjoying various activities. Medieval families engaged in a number of games with their children, such as hide-and-seek and blindman's buff. Another favorite pastime was listening to a good story. Families would gather in the town square and listen to the itinerant minstrel or storyteller. Families often gathered outside their homes on long summer nights to recount the day's events and share a laugh. These were the moments that strengthened the bonds of mutual respect and tenderness in medieval marriages.

Whether medieval marriages came together for business reasons, family agreements, or love, many couples shared affection and mutual respect for each other. Family life consisted of daily chores and pleasurable moments together, however brief. Medieval moralists acknowledged that when wedded couples were compatible and loved each other, their home life was gratifying. This sage observation transcends time and applies to marriages throughout the centuries.

Life in the Castle

John Burke

Medieval castles were self-contained communities during most of the Middle Ages. Medieval warfare centered around the castle, and invading armies had to capture the local castle in order to conquer an area. The castle was also the home to the owner, his family, the knights, and the people who served him.

Towns and villages grew up under the protection of a castle's walls. Markets, fairs, plays, tournaments, and religious ceremonies were held within the castle walls. Inside the castle, life was generally busy even during peaceful times. In the following selection author and historian John Burke reconstructs the everyday living in a medieval castle. He describes the living quarters, stables, chapel, armory, and storerooms. During peacetime, tournaments, hunting expeditions, and lavish feasts were popular pastimes for the residents and guests inside the castle.

The invention of gunpowder by the Chinese and the prohibitive cost of building castles led to a decline in their construction in the late Middle Ages. Having lost their defensive purpose, some castles were turned into palaces by their owners while others were simply abandoned in favor of luxury homes in the growing cities.

Through many generations the great hall was the centre of all castle life, shared by the lord and the majority of his household. Here the business of the estate was largely transacted, here men, women and children slept, and here they ate together. 'It is not seemly,' decreed a medieval book on etiquette, 'that a lord should eat alone.'

Waking in the morning, the lord and his lady would find themselves in their bed at one end of the hall, usually at the back of the dais, curtained off from the rest. Or perhaps they were among the pioneers of what later became customary: a small private chamber partitioned off from the main body of the hall or

John Burke, *Life in the Castle in Medieval England*. New York: British Heritage Press, 1983.

even recessed into the wall of the keep, with wainscoting and some painted panelling to distinguish it from the whitewashed walls elsewhere. If the hall was of the two-storey variety, family bedrooms could be set behind the gallery, and from his solar above the dais the lord was in a position to study activities in the great space below.

Lesser members of his household slept on benches along the walls, upon straw-filled palliasses, or simply on a carpet of rushes and herbs on the floor, pulling cloaks or rugs about them. Since, in spite of regular shifting and replacing, these rushes were all too likely to be impregnated with the grease and spillage from the food consumed in the hall, and with the droppings of favourite dogs and falcons who were present at mealtimes, such a couch must have been none too salubrious. Even in the lord's private recess, carpets were a rarity until well into the thirteenth century, and other luxuries were equally scarce. Tapestries gradually made their appearance, combining pleasant decoration with the need to combat draughts. Early halls had an open fire in the middle of the floor; and even when fireplaces were built into the walls, proper chimneys were unknown until the late thirteenth century, so that the primitive flues driven through the walls combined with draughts from the unglazed windows to swirl a great deal of smoke about, soon discolouring the whitewash.

Morning Duties

The household rose early. The first duty was attendance at mass in the chapel—a small chamber in most early castles, before it became fashionable to sponsor more and more elaborate chapels as prestige symbols. When larger buildings could safely be built within the confines of a reasonably secure bailey, many included a crypt in which generations of the family would be buried. It was rare, though, in Norman times to find anything quite as ambitious as the domestic chapel within the keep at Castle Rising in Norfolk.

Mass was said by the lord's chaplain, or—from the word 'chancel'—chancellor. He would also say grace before meals, and attend to his master's personal and official correspondence.

The first meal of the day was spartan for most: usually a hunk of bread and a pot of ale before work commenced; though the baron himself might have white wheaten bread and a slice of cold meat, perhaps even a glass of wine. While his servants went about their duties, the baron and his steward would then settle down to administrative matters in the hall. Tenants arrived with rents or respectful complaints, submitting local disputes for judgment. There might be ticklish matters of inheritance to settle, or deaths or marriages to discuss. . . .

Mealtime

When the morning's business had been transacted in the hall, the main meal of the day was forthcoming, at what may seem to us the disconcertingly early hour of ten or eleven o'clock. Trestle tables were set up and laid with silver for the lord and his lady on their dais, earthenware vessels and horn or wooden implements for the others. While his retainers sat on the benches which some of them had used for sleeping the night before, the lord and lady might use chairs—imposing but heavy, and through most of the Norman period lacking such comforts as upholstery.

The chaplain said grace. The food was brought in. Because of the difficulty of disposing of smoke and smells, a great deal of cooking was almost certainly done out in the open when weather permitted. Kitchens might be incorporated in buildings against one of the bailey walls, or on the lower floor of the keep with ovens and fireplaces set in the walls, but either way the food was unlikely to arrive very hot at the table after traversing the draughty courtyards or being carried up spiral stone staircases.

The estate and its tenants supplied many ingredients for the various dishes, but in addition there were imported luxuries such as wine and the spices essential to disguise the flavour of bad and rancid meat, fish or soups. With no means of preserving meat other than by salting it down, the practice wherever possible was to eat an animal within a day or so of its being slaughtered; but salting was essential to ensure supplies throughout the winter, since the efficacy of root crops as winter feed had not yet been discovered, or to keep the inmates from starvation during a siege. . . .

At the end of dinner, whether the main course had been meat, fowl, or good red herring, the chaplain's almoner [one who distributes alms for the church] would collect such bones and scraps as had not been tossed to the dogs, and bread left soaking in the bottom of soup bowls. It was his duty to visit the poor and distribute these scraps, and also

> to receive discarded horses, clothing, money and other gifts, bestowed in alms, and to distribute them faithfully. He ought also by frequent exhortations to spur the king to liberal almsgiving, especially on saints' days, and to implore him not to bestow his robes . . . upon players, flatterers, fawners, talebearers or minstrels, but to command them to be used to augment his almsgiving. [From a thirteenth-century document prepared on behalf of the Earl of Chester by his clerk.]

The Lord's Leisure Time

Assuming that the lord of the castle was today spared any such exhortation from his almoner, and that there was no further pressing business to attend to, his mind might well turn to the prospect of an afternoon's hunting. The best days of all were those when there were no administrative duties to be performed and he could set out in the early morning for a whole day in the forest, with a picnic meal to be served during a lull in the chase. Today his treasured falcon had probably been sitting hooded on the back of his chair throughout the meal, and now it was high time to exercise him—or her, for the male tiercel was far less aggressive and less favoured than the female falcon.

To a nobleman, hawking was perhaps the dearest of all aspects of the chase. Deer and wild boar might be pursued avidly through the forests, with the more adventurous ladies accompanying the hunt; but the skilled falconer was the aristocrat of huntsmen, and the falcon more precious than any hunting dog. Animals on the ground could be cornered or worn out before the kill. Birds were more enticingly elusive. There were as yet no guns to massacre them in mid-air, and they could swiftly wing their way out of arrow range. Winged predators had to be trained to swoop on them and bring them down. Training was arduous both for the hawk and hawker, and when it was completed the birds were looked after with the greatest devotion in the castle mews. . . .

On return from the chase the lord might take a bath. Water was poured into a wooden tub in his bedchamber or curtained recess, and he sat in it upon a stool. The soap used would have been made on the premises from meat fat, wood ash and soda, unless he was prepared to import expensive soap from Mediterranean countries, made with an olive oil base and perfumed with herbs.

Shaving must have been an uncomfortable operation with knife blades which, by our standards, were surely jagged and liable to rasp the skin.

Castle Living for the Ladies

In his absence during the afternoon his wife and other ladies of the castle had perhaps worked on their embroidery, gossiped and told tales or riddles, thereafter joining the children when the tutor had released them. Children and adults shared much the same romps and pastimes, including 'hoodman blind' and other variations on blind-man's-buff, skipping and dancing games, and various simple dice games. The more skilled devoted themselves to chess or forms of billiards and backgammon. After supper they might continue in the same mood with the lord joining them or, if he was exhausted by the business and outdoor exercise of his day, retiring to a chamber where some of the ladies might wait on him, flirt with him, and perhaps play music. In the hall other musicians were perhaps tuning up—strolling players to entertain the household and accompany an hour or so of dancing.

With darkness settled down outside, the interior was lit by candles made from wax or animal fat rendered down and then solidified, set on iron-spiked candlesticks or in wall brackets which also held torches of resinous wood or rushlights made from dipping twisted strands of rush into grease or tallow. A portable lantern with its candle shielded by translucent slices of horn was used when negotiating draughty passages or staircases.

When it was time to call an end to the evening, the captain of the guard would ensure that the sentries were properly posted and alert, and the lord and lady retired to their room, said their prayers, hung up their clothes . . . and so to bed.

Private Life in Tuscany

Georges Duby, Dominique Barthélemy, and Charles de la Roncière

In medieval families, the man was head of the house. The woman ran the day-to-day activities of the household. In towns and cities, many men and women worked outside the home. In the villages, men and women toiled in the fields from sunrise to sunset. Women in both cities and villages also had numerous duties (such as cleaning, washing, cooking, and collecting firewood) to attend to within the household. Children were expected to help their mothers with household chores.

Medieval families worked hard most of the time, but they did allow time to spend together. Finding spare time in a busy day was not always easy, especially in the summer when the workdays were longer. The early sunset of winter shortened the workday and gave the medieval family a respite from labor; they could gather around the hearth, sip warm ale or wine, and tell a few stories.

Georges Duby, Dominique Barthélemy, and Charles de la Roncière present a slice of life in a medieval Tuscan family. Many medieval historians have presented medieval families as downtrodden and disinterested in family life. This viewpoint is not accurate. As the selection illustrates, medieval people allowed leisure time to spend with their family in the midst of all their laboring. The family meal was the most important time of day. Many times, mealtime was the only chance the family had to be together to laugh and talk. Private family time was important to medieval people, and from the dawn of the Middle Ages to the close of the Middle Ages, family ties continued to remain strong.

Duby was a noted historian and lecturer of medieval studies. Barthélemy was an old testament scholar. De la Roncière was a historian of exploration and cartography.

Georges Duby, Dominique Barthélemy, and Charles da la Roncière, *A History of Private Life: Revelations of the Medieval World,* edited by Georges Duby and translated by Arthur Goldhammer. Cambridge, MA: The Belknap Press of Harvard University Press, 1988.

Shopkeepers and craftsmen usually worked outside the home. In Florence most artisans rented workshops in a different part of the city from where they lived. Instances are known in which workshop and residence were combined, but these were rare. During the day working people left their homes—men, women, and even children (who began work, in some cases, as early as age eight or ten). Some trades were traditionally practiced at home, however: weaving (practiced by both men and women) and above all spinning (practiced by women). Inventories of woolworkers' furniture (1378) often include a loom and a *filatoio*, or spinning wheel; these work-related items were listed along with the furniture and installed in private residences. The same was true in Siena in the mid-fifteenth century and in many other places. When husband and wife were both weavers or the husband was a weaver and the wife a spinner, they could work together at home throughout the day and sometimes late into the night. In the countryside work was even more inseparable from private life. In the cities it was quite rare for families to work together at home and more of a threat than a boon to family intimacy, for work could easily swallow up both day and night, especially in poor households.

Home Life

Fortunately there was no lack of opportunity for family members who dispersed for work in the morning to spend time together in the evening when work was done (at vespers in the case of Florentine masons) or all day long on Sundays and holidays.

Washing was one good opportunity for seeing other family members. The mother supervised the washing of the children (according to Giovanni Dominici [fourteenth-century author and moralist]). When adults washed, they were not always alone, and the early morning hours were not the only ones reserved for doing one's toilette. It was normal for a wife to assist in her husband's ablutions. Matrons had servants help them wash (at least their feet), dress, and put on makeup. Mutual delousing was so common among the ladies of Ravenna that a thirteenth-century regulation forbade anyone from engaging in the activity under public arcades.

Family members were together at and sometimes before meals. At Fiesole [town near Florence], in July 1338, an observer sketched a housewife preparing the evening soup while her fifteen-year-old daughter sat on a low chest, her elder daughter sat in the doorway with her chin on her knees waiting for her beau, and a young rascal of a son paced up and down. Eventually all sat down for dinner. Eating together was both an ideal, as Alberti [fourteenth-century moralist] reminds us, and a reality. Rich or poor, Florentine households owned at least one table, either rectangular and mounted on trestles or round, and obviously used at mealtimes. (Some inventories are explicit: "round dining table," for example.) Storytellers take it for granted that husbands and wives eat together, probably along with children above a certain age. Servants did not eat with the family, except possibly in rural and relatively modest urban homes.

Private Conversations

After supper the family's evening began. There was much work for everyone, including daily chores such as shelling beans, scouring, mending, cleaning, and repairs. There was also a great deal to say; evenings were for conversation, as they are everywhere. People discussed their daily labor: they talked "sheep, wheat, buildings, and other usual topics of married couples," according to a witness reporting the conversation of a peasant couple. They discussed their plans for the future, such as whom their daughter should marry, and their worries: oppressive taxes, children who were born one after another and "did nothing but eat," and all the other complaints that one can read about in the tax declarations, which record so many tales of woe and echoes of marital squabbles. Some conversations were absorbed by such matters as a daughter's dowry, possible investments, and (in the case of sharecroppers) relations with the landlord or patron. Moralists complained about the licentiousness of private conversation, but there was also talk of religion. Even the most pious and well-bred families were at times shaken by moments of anger in which each member "exhaled his bitterness in violent words," as Saint Catherine's biographer said of her family. Grandparents sometimes recalled their childhood and discussed the family genealogy (not always with great confidence). There was outraged comment on local scandals: bigamy, murder, clerical misconduct, and so on. All these examples are taken from fourteenth-century Tuscan sources. The range of conversation among the humanists and the urban bourgeoisie was naturally broader, but on occasion even they chatted about the simple matters of daily life. Alberti praised the charm of relaxed conversation about "cattle, wool, vines, and seeds," in which vacation permitted him to indulge. But he could rise to whatever heights the occasion demanded. At the home of one of his uncles, "the custom was never to speak of futile things, always of magnificent ones." In real or imaginary dialogues the humanists liked to display their erudition.

Family Leisure Time

In addition to conversation there were games: dice (frowned upon), chess (often mentioned in bourgeois homes), and, later, cards. Or the children might be called in (Palmieri [fourteenth-century historian] tells us) for alphabet games. When they were a little older, there was evening reading, as in the home of the dignified and pious notary Lapo Mazzei of Prato, who spent winter evenings reading Saint Francis' *Fioretti* to his children (1390). A hundred years later (1485), an uncle of the young humanist prodigy Michele Verini read to him from the Bible after dinner (and from Euclid for an apéritif).

The structure of the house, not all parts of which were equally well heated (or cooled), lent itself to evening gatherings. During the summer the family often sat together on the steps or in the garden or in various kinds of loggias. In winter everyone gathered around the fire in the *sala*, as the wife read and the master talked and kept the fire going, while the children sat on stools in a variety of attitudes, listening—the scene formed the subject of innumerable illuminations. On certain occasions, such as the birth of a child or a case of illness, the family gathered in the bedroom. To purists, however, this was an encroachment upon space that properly belonged to the lady of the house or the couple; in their eyes the place for family socializing was the living room. This certainly had its role, but a nuclear family—married couple and children—was probably more comfortable in the warmer, more intimate surroundings of the bedroom. The great halls of bourgeois houses were used mainly to receive large numbers of relatives and guests, while only a select few were allowed access to the bedrooms.

A Love Letter to a Wife

Richard Calle

Marriage in the Middle Ages was a partnership that had little to do with romantic love; although a few did marry for love, they were the exception. The main purposes of marriage were financial security and procreation. Nobles arranged marriages for their children to partners of equal or greater wealth. The average age for a noble girl to marry was twelve years old. A noble girl's husband would be considerably older and wealthier than she. Peasants married at a later age since acquisition of land for the man and a suitable dowry for the woman were required before they married. Peasant men married in their late twenties, and peasant women, a few years younger.

In the following selection, a letter written during the late Middle Ages, a man professes his love for his wife. The letter was written by Richard Calle to Margery Paston. Paston was the daughter of a well-to-do family in Norfolk, England. Calle was a servant in the Paston household. He and Margery fell in love and secretly wed. When Margery's brother, John Paston III, found out about the marriage, he confined Margery in the family home and placed her under strict scrutiny. In the letter, Calle writes of his love for his bride and of his distress on their separation.

My own lady and mistress, and before God my true wife, I with heart full sorrowful recommend me to you as one that cannot be merry nor shall be until it be otherwise with us than it is now; for this life that we lead now is no pleasure to God or to the world, considering the great bond of matrimony that is made between us, and also the great love that has been and I trust yet is between us, and on my part never greater.

Wherefore I beseech Almighty God to comfort us as soon as it pleases Him, for we that ought by right to be most together are most asunder; it seems a thousand years ago since I spoke with you. I had rather be with you than have all the goods in the

Richard Calle, *A Medieval Family: The Pastons of Fifteenth-Century England*, edited by Frances and Joseph Gies. New York: HarperPerennial, 1998.

world. Also, alas! good lady, they that keep us thus asunder remember full little what they do.

I understand, lady, you have had as much sorrow for me as any gentlewoman has had in the world, as would God all the sorrow that you have had had rested upon me, so that you had been discharged of it, for I know, lady, it is to me a death to hear that you are treated otherwise than you ought to be [confined to her home by her brother]. This is a painful life that we lead. I cannot live thus without its being a great displeasure to God.

Also like you to know that I had sent you a letter from London by my lad [his servant], and he told me he could not speak with you, there was made so great a watch upon him and you both. He told me John Thresher [a friend of the Paston family] came to him from you, and said that you sent him for a letter or a token from me, but my lad trusted him not. . . . Alas, what do they mean! I suppose they think we are not contracted [married] together, and if they do, I marvel, for then they are not well advised, remembering the plainness with which I broke [the matter] to . . . . Margaret [Margery's mother] at the beginning, and I suppose you too, if you did as you ought to have done; and if you have done the contrary [deny the marriage], as I have been informed, you did not do it according to conscience or for the pleasure of God, unless you did it out of fear, and for the moment to please those that were around you; and if you did it for this purpose, it was a reasonable cause, considering the great and importunate pressure on you, and that many an untrue tale was told to you about me, which God knows I was never guilty of.

My lad told me that . . . your mother asked him if he had brought my letter to you, and many other things she insinuated. . . . I know not what [your mother] . . . means, for by my troth there is no gentlewoman alive that my heart is more tender for than her, or is more loath to displace, saving only yourself. . . . I suppose if you tell them plainly the truth, they would not damn their souls for us; though when I tell them the truth, they will not believe me as well as they will do you; and therefore, good lady, at the reverence of God, be plain to them, and tell the truth, and if they will in no wise agree thereto, between God and the Devil and them be it. . . .

I marvel much that they should take this matter [their marriage] so hard as I understand they do, remembering that it is in such as it cannot be remedied, and my deserts in every way are such that there should be no obstacle against it. . . . Mistress, I am afraid to write to you, for I understand you have showed my letters that I have sent you before this time; but I pray you let no creature see this letter. As soon as you have read it, let it be burnt, for I would no man should see it; you have had no writing from me this two years, and I will send you no more; Jesus preserve, keep, and give you your heart's desire, which I know well should be God's pleasure.

This letter was written with as great pain as ever a thing I wrote in my life, for in good faith I have been right sick, and yet am not verily well, God amend it.

Home and Furnishings

Geneviève D'Haucourt

Medieval homes were sparsely furnished, poorly lighted, cold, and very drafty. Peasants shared their homes with their livestock. Their homes were built of mud, thatch roofs, and earth floors covered in straw. Townspeople had homes built of wood with narrow windows covered in oiled linen cloth. Wealthy people had homes built of stone with glass windows and shutters. All styles of homes were furnished with a table, a few chairs, a trunk, and a bed for the richer classes. Nobles covered their walls in tapestries to help keep out the cold. The floor plans of the poor, middle, and rich classes were basically the same: All had a large room in which people worked, cooked, ate, slept, and entertained. In the following selection French historian Geneviève D'Haucourt meticulously describes the typical housing of persons ranging from laborers to kings. D'Haucourt was an archivist-paleographer at the Ecole des Chartes in Paris.

We know quite a lot about medieval housing, especially as quite a few examples of it remain today.

The plan was simple: There was a large room for people to live in. Working, cooking, eating, sleeping and entertaining were all carried on in the one room, much as still happens on some farms today. Both country people and town dwellers—even lords and high-ranking princes—lived in this way, the only difference being that whereas the houses of the poor were built of mud, those of the rich were of stone.

Moreover, besides the living quarters there had to be a wine cellar, a granary, a threshing barn, a shed for the hay and carts, a stable, mangers and a pigsty. A rural dwelling, whether belonging to a noble or a laborer, was therefore surrounded with farm buildings, whose number and size depended on the wealth of the land and therefore on that of the householder.

This simple plan was altered or elaborated on when the way

Geneviève D'Haucourt, *Life in the Middle Ages*, translated by Veronica Hull and Christopher Fernau. New York: Walter and Company, 1963.

of life was not purely a family one. For a larger number of people it was necessary either to provide separate places to live or to keep different rooms for different functions.

The first solution was adopted by the kings and nobles: St. Louis often ate and held court in his room, and his knights slept at the foot of his bed. Under his room and connected with it by a little private staircase was the queen's room, where she lived with her ladies-in-waiting. Thus the most important members of the household had their own quarters, where they lived with their attendants. The kitchen formed a separate domain. Inhabited by the hierarchy of servants. Separate, too, was the great hall, where the king could hold audience, preside over an assembly, or give a banquet.

The second solution was adopted by the monasteries, where there was a common dormitory (sometimes separated into cells, sometimes not), a refectory, a chapel, a chapter hall, a library, a kitchen and guest quarters.

In the towns, where space was scarce and land dear, it was necessary to build upward rather than outward. Each household generally had its own house. For the artisan there was sometimes a cellar, and a room on the ground floor that was both workshop and shop; sometimes there was room for a kitchen and dining room at the back, with the same chimney serving both rooms. On the first floor, which led into the street by a straight flight of stairs, was the room where everything went on. On the second was the granary, or several small rooms connected with the main room by either an interior stairway or a spiral stairway that gave on to the courtyard. The plan was based on a rectangle whose shorter side faced the street. It could be modified to suit people with more money or more sophisticated tastes; for instance, there could be a dressing room off the main room. In the fourteenth century a separate dining room was provided. Collectors had libraries, each castle had a chapel and smaller houses had an oratory.

Lastly, palaces—such as that of the Comtesse d'Artois—had special quarters where guests or the public could amuse themselves with various devices and tricks—apparatus nowadays confined to the fairground.

Building materials varied according to the district, the means of the prospective owner, and the builder's custom. There was

Many former serfs moved to towns where they could earn a living by practicing a trade. Above their shops, they built modest living quarters.

quarry stone, freestone, cob and clay to choose from. The timber was well constructed, light and solid, and was made from heart of oak, which the insects could not damage. The roof was made from slate, slats of shale or lava, round or flat tiles, or timber or thatch. There were no gutters at the edge of the roof, but the larger buildings had gargoyles.

The ground floor inside was often flagged, and the planked ceiling formed the floor of the room above. The floors of peasant houses and of granaries were usually made of dirt.

Light came in at the windows, which were sometimes very

small but could also be so large as to take up almost the whole of the wall facing the street. The streets were very narrow, and it was necessary to get as much light as possible. There were few window panes except in churches; other windows were made of oiled or waxed cloth or paper, wood or willow lattice. There were wooden shutters outside the ground-floor windows and inside the upstairs ones.

The chimneys were large, usually built against the wall in the kitchen and the main rooms, and there was a stone bench under the mantelpiece. English halls, however, retained to the end of the Middle Ages the round-shaped open fireplace in the middle of the room. The smoke was said to be beneficial to the roof timbers and to the lungs of the dwellers. In the kitchen was a sink with a pipe that led outside. As for water, it had to be brought from the well on the premises, from the local well, or from a fountain.

Lavatories were a convenience that architects were careful to supply in abundance. The ideal, achieved in certain castles and religious houses, was to have as many lavatories as beds. The lavatories were, where possible, small sheds jutting out of the wall and giving on to a river (where there was one), or on to a cesspool, which was sometimes filled with deodorizing and antiseptic charcoal. In Paris the lavatories gave on to a soil-tub, but it seems that there was some difficulty in insuring the regular emptying of these, owing to the lack of volunteers for the work. . . .

Home Security

The need for security in a country open to attack meant that the men of the Middle Ages had to fortify their homes or find a safe place to go if necessary. The first type of defense was the moat, whose ramp was topped with a fence of plaited thorn or bramble; such a fortified place was called in French a *plessis*. Later on there were stone walls, and the place was called a castle (a fortified house or village) or a fortified town (a more important and larger group of dwellings).

Strategic and economic reasons dictated that the houses encircled by this expensive means of defense be built close together, upward rather than outward, and with only narrow streets between them. In England—apart from the very centers, which were usually congested—there remained considerable free space in the towns, since most of them were fortified at a late date or with inexpensive means, such as a dirt bank and ditch; but elsewhere the only empty space was the cemetery near the church, a few tiny squares on one of which stood the pillory, the monastery gardens and the courtyards of private houses. Even the bridges were built upon: in London, Paris, York, Bristol; and the houses on the Ponte Vecchio in Florence are still standing. . . .

Home Furnishings

The furniture of the medieval house was as simple as the house itself; there was not much of it, and it often consisted only of a bed and a chest or cupboard rough-hewn from thick planks.

The bed was usually large, because it had to accommodate from two to six people. (The daughters of the ogre in "Tom Thumb" slept in a medieval bed.) In the case of the very poor the bed was a container filled with hay, a sack of straw serving as a bolster. But most people had a straw pallet covered with one or more feather mattresses; "to sleep on a bed of feathers" expressed the height of comfort.

Over the mattresses there were sheets of linen or hemp, fine or crude according to the owner's purse or the skill of his wife. Even so, some of the very poor and some monasteries did without linen altogether and only used blankets of serge. (In such cases people slept fully dressed, except for the cloak and topcoat.) The sheets were not tucked in but hung at the sides of the bed—as is still done in Germany—or right down to the floor. The bolster was covered with the lower sheet, and the upper sheet was turned back, as it is today, over the blankets. These were generally made of serge. In the winter there were furred covers of ermine or squirrel for the rich, and for the common people there were coverlets lined with fox or rabbit fur. There were also quilted coverlets stuffed with wool or feathers.

The chest or cupboard often stood on four feet, at least when it had to rest on a dirt floor, and it served the double purpose of cupboard and seat. Clothes were kept in it—carefully rolled and scattered with iris root, lavender or saffron, as is still done in certain districts—and also papers and parchments (deeds, receipts and loans) and money tied up in a leather pouch or canvas bag.

The cupboard was often finished off with heavy ironwork and one or two imposing locks. But its owner took good care to keep it beside his bed, or, if it was a small one containing only the most precious objects and papers, under his bed. In this way he made sure that he would not be robbed in the night. In the larger houses, where the wardrobe had a special place of its own off the main room, the boxes of money and clothes were often stored inside it.

For those who could manage it, there was a table, usually standing on trestles, which meant it could be cleared away after use (today we "clear the table" after a meal; for the Middle Ages, the expression was a literal one). When the table was a dormant one (mostly in kitchens or dining rooms used only for the one purpose), there were often several three- or four-legged wooden stools kept under it.

Seating Arrangements

As for seating, apart from these stools there were one or two large chairs, which were kept for the head of the household or the most important people present (in an important kitchen they would be used by the master cooks). Also there were benches, which were chests with backs to them, covered with cushions; these were used by the most important people in the family or by guests.

In the thirteenth century many households were still short of things to sit on. They used trusses of straw that could be covered with some fine material for an honored guest or for general use in a household with luxurious habits. Students attended lectures sitting on bundles of straw; but a contemporary novel depicts an emperor's daughter seated in a room with her attendants on straw trusses covered with material on which coats of arms were embroidered, and leaning against a bed that served as a backrest. This sort of seat had the advantage of being warm in winter.

The churches had cupboards, too, some of them very large, as may be seen in the cathedrals of Bayeux and Evreux; these were also to be found in private houses from the fourteenth century on.

Rich houses completed their furnishing with tapestries, which could be changed to provide a different décor, or which could be carried about on the frequent moves in a nobleman's life to re-create a home. In winter the tapestries prevented drafts; they also served to divide a large communal room into several smaller rooms, in the same way as Japanese screens do.

Floor Coverings and Kitchenware

On the floor there were sometimes skins, but often straw in the winter, and rushes, gladioli and aromatic plants (mint, verbena and so forth) in the summer. The royal palace, after a general cleaning, would send its discarded straw to the hospital.

Domestic utensils were few in type but many in number, at least in the fourteenth century, when each household was the center of a family craft. The crockery was usually simple earthenware or pewter, and consisted of bowls shared by two people for liquid food, plates, spoons and pitchers for the drink, and also wooden utensils—tankards and small casks for the precious wines and spirits, plates and spoons. The kitchen was furnished much the same as a rural kitchen in some parts of Europe today. In it was a tripod—because the cooking was done on the hearth—one or more earthenware or iron pots, an iron skillet, a ladle; also a pestle and mortar for the preparation of sauces (especially from garlic, which was one of the most important seasonings of the medieval kitchen). The richer houses had more of these basic utensils, and added to them grills, copper pots, firedogs and spits.

There was usually a tub in the kitchen for the laundry and for taking baths, some barrels, a cask or huge pot for the bacon, an ax to split wood, buckets, a shovel, brooms, a warming pan and often a kneading trough.

With this equipment the meals for the family were prepared, either from what was raised in the garden or from the produce of the district bought at the market. The peasant tended to be entirely self-sufficient, having his own wheat for bread, bacon, preserves, salted or smoked meat, jam, honey, spirits, ale, beer, wine, linen and other materials—all made in the house from what was grown on his land. This way of life persisted, in French Canada, down to 1860.

Medieval Clothing

Douglas Gorsline

The fashions of the Middle Ages went through many changes. The earlier fashions were reminiscent of ancient Greek and Roman styles, with flowing togas and short wraps. Beginning in A.D. 1100 clothing became longer for women and shorter for men. Men regularly wore muslim tunic shirts with tights, and the women wore long dresses with tights. Medieval women wore headdresses that proclaimed the wearer's social identity (simple hair wraps for the peasants; silk, embroidered caps for the middle class; and elaborate jeweled, veiled, and tall headgear for the rich). Author Douglas Gorsline, who is a noted illustrator, etcher, and painter, describes the fashion changes of the medieval wardrobe for men and women.

When the Romans arrived in England they found men and women fully clothed and well protected against the cold climate. Men wore sleeved, short-skirted coats and loose trousers, with cloaks and simple hats for colder weather. They also had tightly fitting leather garments and furs. Women's ankle-length gowns were covered by an outer short tunic. These people were dyers as well as weavers. They wore colored garments and massive gold armbands, rings, brooches, and pins. Men had no armor, but their tightly woven felt coverings were almost swordproof.

Across the Channel pre-Norman dress was also simple. Men wore short, loose, sleeveless smocks or tunics caught at the waist with leather thongs; Gallic breeches, tied around the waist; and as hose, either fabric or an extension of the breeches cross-gartered below the knee. A calf-length mantle, fastened at the shoulder, usually covered the head, but hats and caps were rare. Ankle-height shoes had pointed tabs in front and behind. Nobles' tunics and shoes were embroidered with silk or yarn. After the time of Charlemagne (*d.* 814) the men wore their hair short. Women's long gowns covered their feet; the sleeves were loose and some-

Douglas Gorsline, *What People Wore: A Visual History of Dress from Ancient Times to Twentieth-Century America.* New York: Bonanza Books, 1952.

times extended as low as the knee. Over this garment a shorter tunic was worn. Mantles were either long or short; sometimes they were hooded, and the point of the hood could be wrapped around the chin. Fine gloves and handkerchiefs were used.

In battle a ruler would be completely armored, and even the common soldier had metal armlets, helmet, leg protection, and shield.

When the Normans invaded Britain they adopted some fashions, such as that of wearing long hair and beards, which they carried back to the Continent; but in general Norman dress was taken over by the Britons. With William II (reigned 1087–1100) there was an increase in luxuriousness of clothing. Long cloaks and trailing gowns with sleeves falling far below the level of the hands were adopted, and boots and shoes became exaggeratedly sharp-pointed. Both men and women had long and flowing hair; men's beards gradually became less common.

The period of the Crusades acquainted Europeans for the first time with the East, and it is not surprising that many Oriental influences are noted at this time. In the twelfth century men wore not only long, loose-skirted outer and under tunics with tightly laced, fitted bodices, but also undershirts of linen to which the long hose were attached. A woman's tunic was similar but longer; under this was a linen undergarment, the chemise. By the end of this century an ample fur-lined overgarment, the pelisson, had been adopted by men and women. Hoods were much in use, lengthened at the back to a long point, the liripipe.

During the thirteenth century a comparatively simple cloak became the dominant dress form. Among the upper classes rich furs, silk, or cloth of gold served as linings. Under the cloak was a garment best described as a simple gown; its sleeves were often wide, cut short to show the narrower and longer sleeves of an undergarment. This same basic gown was also worn by working people, but in their case it was cut off at the knees to permit manual labor. Hoods or tight caps tied under the chin were commonly worn by men and women; women also often draped the hair with a piece of fabric that fell to the shoulders.

The basic dress remained rectangular until the late fourteenth and the fifteenth centuries, when society was more sophisticated and complex. Clothing gradually abandoned simple lines and assumed the fantastic richness and elaborateness associated with the later medieval period.

Men's gowns became shorter but still covered the knees. A tailored doublet was developed, and in the second half of the fourteenth century the cote-hardie was imported from Germany. This was a low-necked, laced or buttoned outer garment. It grew shorter and by the middle of the fifteenth century was little more than frockcoat length. The houppelande then became the fashion; this was a long, loose tunic, usually belted, with fitted shoulders, high collar, and flowing sleeves. As materials and workmanship improved, hose became longer and the doublet correspondingly shorter. Sleeves and hem lines were frequently "slittered" or jagged, which gave to clothing much of its opulent, fantastic character. Men's and women's hair was often garlanded with jeweled cloth, and there was great variety in hats, caps, and hoods. Buttons were becoming popular and might adorn a garment or sleeve from top to bottom, quite apart from function.

Women of rank wore loose, trailing gowns, but they also borrowed the men's styles of cote-hardie and houppelande. The feminine modification of the latter had a short-waisted bodice and a belted, gored skirt which often trailed behind. Women's clothing was frequently decorated with heraldric motifs, in the manner of men's armorial bearings.

The Late Middle Ages

At the beginning of the fifteenth century man's usual garment was a loose, pleated tunic either lined or edged with fur. Long and baggy sleeves, drawn in tightly at the wrists, were often buttoned. Underneath was another shorter tunic or doublet with close-fitting sleeves fastened at the wrists. A cloak and hood or a hooded cloak was worn over all. A loose girdle belted the waist; suspended from it was the anlace or baselard—the tapering short sword or dagger of the period. Shoes were still exaggeratedly pointed. Many kinds of hats and caps were worn, most of them derivatives of the hood and liripipe of the preceding century. One of the more bizarre styles consisted of a circular roll of cloth bound about the brow and descending on both sides in folds cascading to the shoulder or even to the waist. Everything contributed to an appearance of casual magnificence at once lordly and elegant. As the century drew to a close, the points of shoes became less noticeable and finally disappeared, while the soles broadened and gradually became stubby during the reign of Henry VIII. The dangles from the girdle became tokens: first a purse, later even beads. By the end of the century hose reached to the waistline and the codpiece, introduced earlier in the century, was increasingly evident.

Women adopted men's furred tunics, but their gowns were longer. The gown had a skin-tight bodice, was girdled high under the breasts, and then fell loosely to the ground in wide folds. Sleeves either buttoned tightly or were prolonged as tippets extending far below the hands. A long and plain cloak fastened at the breast with a cord. Religious practices influenced the covering of the hair: cauls were drawn up and around the head into shapes such as hearts or horns; in some, fantastic wired arrangements caused the cambric veiling or wimple to float out behind like a butterfly. By the latter part of the century, however, clothing had become more severe and sensible: skirts no longer dragged on the ground, necks were higher, and sleeves, for the most part, were elbow length.

Medieval Armor

European armor evolved roughly over the thousand years from 650 to 1650, but in the defensive accouterment of ancient peoples can be found the forerunner for practically everything later developed. Not only Greek and Roman influences can be traced, but Etruscan, Celtic, and Byzantine. Etruscan bronze helmets, for example, date from well before the twelfth century B.C.

Defensive armor in the early feudal period was not elaborate. The knight's lower legs were unprotected. Over his torso he wore a hawberk, or tunic, of chain mail slashed at the bottom to fasten about the thigh. A conical steel helmet with a nose guard protected his face. He carried a kite-shaped shield about four feet long.

It must be remembered that armor was, on the whole, the prerogative of the upper classes. The suits of steel commonly seen in museums were worn only by the greatest and wealthiest of lords, and rarely, if at all, by the common fighting men of the Middle Ages. The ordinary soldier was fortunate if he had a tunic of mail and a steel cap. Many of those who aspired to knighthood had to remain squires, or servants to knights, because of their inability to afford the chivalric glory of full armor.

Beginning with the twelfth century, chain mail was gradually extended to include hood and hose, clothing the knight from head to foot. Under the mail was a gambeson, and over it a pourpoint, both made of leather or quilted fabric. The problem of distinguishing friend from foe, when both were completely encased in steel, was solved by the introduction, in the twelfth century, of amorial bearings, which laid the foundation for the great arts and skills of heraldry.

During the thirteenth century chain mail was gradually reinforced by plates at strategic points, beginning with the chest region. The great helm was common, but its use was reserved chiefly for tournaments and display. In battle the knight wore a mail hood with a steel cap either over or under it. Helms were of great variety, some flat or round-topped with a hinged or movable ventaile (to admit air), and others in one piece, pierced for eye holes. At the end of the century the sugarloaf shape of helm was introduced.

By the fourteenth century the knight was entirely encased in plate metal having articulated joints. The characteristic helmet of this time was the salade, a large steel cap visored all around. The toes of metal shoes were sharply pointed.

Armor of the fifteenth century was simpler in construction and therefore somewhat lighter in weight. A shirt of light mail was worn as additional protection under the plate. As this century progressed, however, armor ceased to be functional and began to imitate civilian clothing.

The sixteenth century continued this trend and in addition emphasized decoration; surface etching and inlay provided the final corruption of the beautiful lines and utility of earlier armor. Incidentally, the decoration of armor gave impetus to the art of etching. The introduction of gunpowder doomed utilitarian armor. At first, in order to protect the wearer against powder-driven shot, armor was made heavier, but, as its weight became impractical, it was gradually abandoned. This transition period, during which firearms were becoming practical weapons and the armorer was concerned chiefly with ostentatious display, lasted into the seventeenth century. After that time the preoccupations of fighting men were devoted to weapons of offense rather than of defense.

Community and Work

Chapter Preface

The medieval church was integral to the daily life of villagers, townspeople, and city dwellers. For common people, the church was the unifying force during an unstable time. The parish church united villagers, and the elaborate cathedrals united town and city people.

Each village had a parish church, where the parish priest lived and celebrated weekly Mass. In some villages, the lord of the manor built the church and hired the priest himself. In these instances, the lord, and not the centralized church, owned the parish and was entitled to all revenues it generated. If he cared to, the lord could sell or bequeath the church. The ownership of the parish church did not matter to the general population. What mattered to the masses was that the parish was always open to them. The parish priest was the most important person in the church organization. It was essential for everyone to participate in the sacraments—baptism and holy communion—as well as confirmation (receiving the Holy Spirit), penance, and the last rites (anointing of the dying or dead). Without engaging in these rituals, there was no hope of eternal life.

The parish church was not only a place for religious worship; it was also a place for socializing. Here, baptisms were rejoiced, marriages were celebrated, and deaths were mourned. It was also the center of village life, where weekly markets and town meetings were held and annual fairs took place. The parish clergy were drawn heavily from the peasantry, and their learning was slight; however, the hearing of confessions, the offering of the sacraments, and the functioning of the penitential system on the local level had an enormous impact on society.

The town and city people also found comfort in their parishes. Ornate, multitowered cathedrals replaced the simple structure of the village church. The twelfth and thirteenth centuries saw a burst of architectural design in the building of the great cathedrals of Europe. Notre Dame in Paris and Canterbury Cathedral in London are two of the splendid cathedrals built during the Middle Ages.

Like the village church, the cathedrals were integral to daily living. People attended Mass, vespers (prayers), ceremonies (baptisms, weddings), and events (town meetings, markets, and fairs) at the cathedral. The house of God was by far the largest building in the town or city, thus making it the most logical place for public meetings and events. Cathedrals were the skyscrapers of their day. For example, Notre Dame stood at 110 feet high (about ten stories) and towered over the city, dwarfing all surrounding buildings.

For the town and city dweller, life was more material and hectic than for the villager. Even in the midst of the bustling markets, the cathedral's bells reverberated throughout the streets, and people were reminded again of the importance the church had in their lives. The church and daily life were intricately woven together to form a thread between the physical and the spiritual world. Religion was everywhere; it was the core of existence and the core of everyday living. Medieval people could not conceive a world without prayers, atonement, and their local priest. The church provided Europe with a common religious and cultural unity. This unity persisted well after the Middle Ages came to a close.

English Village Life

Robert Lacey and Danny Danziger

In the early Middle Ages (approximately A.D. 500 to A.D. 1100) most western Europeans lived in the countryside. Villages of about ten to twelve homes dotted the landscape throughout most of Europe. These settlements were constantly open to attack by invaders (Vikings, Visigoths, and Germanic tribes). Peasants were unable to fight off the invaders, thus paving the way for a new political and economic way of life—the manorial system.

The owner of the manor was from the noble class. He owned large estates of land (manor) and had labor (serfs and free peasants) toil the land for him. The peasants, in exchange for the land, owed the lord a fixed rent in money or crop. The lord was obliged to protect the peasants on his manor. Serfs were either descendants of slaves from the Roman Empire or formerly free peasants who descended into serfdom due to poverty or the need for protection from the lord. Although serfs were required to work the lord's land, they could grow their own crops. Out of these crops, the serf paid the lord a fee and kept what was left. This system was a very small improvement over slavery; nevertheless, the serf was able to gain a small bit of economic independence.

In the following selection best-selling author Robert Lacey and award-winning interviewer Danny Danziger explore village life at the turn of the first millennium. Lacey, author of *The Men and the Machine*, and Danziger, whose interviews have appeared in the London *Sunday Times*, delve into everyday life for the peasant in the year A.D. 1000. As the Middle Ages progressed, the manorial system deepened its hold on the serfs and "free" peasants until the growth of cities and commerce weakened it. By the end of the Middle Ages the manorial system had crumbled.

It was the quietness of life in a medieval English village that would most strike a visitor from today—no planes overhead, no swish or rumble from traffic. Stop reading this book a minute.

Robert Lacey and Danny Danziger, *The Year 1000: What Life Was Like at the Turn of the First Millennium: An Englishman's World*. New York: Little, Brown and Company, 1999.

Can you hear something? Some machine turning? A waterpipe running? A distant radio or a pneumatic drill digging up the road? Of all the varieties of modern pollution, noise is the most insidious.

Yet in the year 1000 the hedgerows actually had a sound. You could hear baby birds chirping in their nests, and the only mechanical noise you would hear came from the wheezing of the blacksmith's bellows. In some villages you might have heard the bell in the church tower, or the creaking and clunking of the wooden cogs in one of the water mills that had been constructed in the last 2000 years, and if you lived near one of England's dozen or so cathedrals, you would have heard the heavy metal cascadings of sound from the copper windpipes of one of the recently imported church organs. But that was all. As bees buzzed and wood pigeons cooed, you could listen to God's creation and take pleasure in its subtle variety.

The year 1000 was an empty world, with much more room to stretch out and breathe. With a total English population of little more than a million, there was just one person for every forty or fifty with whom we are surrounded today, and most people lived in small communities, a couple of dozen or so homes circling a village green or extending up and down a single, winding street—the archetypal little village or hamlet to which the modern suburban cul-de-sac pays nostalgic homage. The centuries leading up to 1000 A.D. were the years in which people picked out the crossroads, valley, or stream-crossing where they thought they could piece together a living. Villages built around a green may originally have been constructed in a circular pattern to provide protection for livestock against wolves or other marauders. By the end of the first millennium almost every modern English village existed and bore its modern name, and these names can tell us whether the identity of that village was primarily shaped by the Anglo-Saxons or the Danes.

Place names ending in *ham*, the Old English for "settlement," indicate an Anglo-Saxon origin—as in Durham, Clapham, or Sandringham. Other Anglo-Saxon endings include *ing* (as in Reading), *stowe* (as in Felixstowe), *stead* (as in Hampstead), and *ton* (as in Kingston). Viking settlements can be identified by the ending *by*, which originally meant a farm (as in Whitby, Derby, or Grimsby); and other Danish endings include *thorpe* (as in Scunthorpe), *toft,* meaning a plot of land (as in Lowestoft), and *scale,* meaning a temporary hut or shelter (as in Windscale). . . .

Through the Eyes of the Villager

The village where he lived was the beginning and almost the end of the Englishman's world. He knew that he lived in Engla-lond, and he probably knew the name of the king whose crude image was stamped on the coins that were starting to play quite a role in the village economy. He would have also made excursions to the tops of the nearest hills to gaze out on other villages which he might have visited, and he had almost certainly made his way to the nearest market town along one of the deep, sunken tracks that wound their way between the fields.

As he stood on the hilltop, he would not have seen significantly more woodland than we would today. It is frequently supposed that medieval England was clad in thick forests, but Neolithic Britons had started cutting down trees and growing crops as early as 5000 B.C., and the Romans were major land managers, laying down villas and farms, as well as their roads, across the countryside. Anglo-Saxon plough teams continued the process, so an Anglo-Saxon standing on the top of, say, Box Hill in Surrey in the year 1000 would have looked out on a pattern of vegetation that was little different from that surveyed by Jane Austen's Emma eight hundred years later.

That Anglo-Saxon would also have seen one or two of the bright, new stone parish churches that were to become the heart of English village life in the second millennium. England's earliest Christian missionaries were monks who went out from the cathedral abbeys to preach at the foot of the tall crosses that survive in the centre of a few ancient towns and villages today. The tall cross marked the point where the people of the village gathered to pray, but as the church grew richer, congregations were able to build themselves houses of worship, first in wood and later in stone.

The Englishman's own home was certainly a wooden structure, based on a framework of sturdy beams stuck into the ground and fastened together with wooden pegs. This framework was then covered in planks or served as the basis for a heavy, basket-like weaving of willow or hazel branches that were covered in "cob"—a mixture of clay, straw, and cow dung that was used until quite recent times for the construction of cottages in Somerset and Devon. Roofs were thatched with straw or reeds, while windows were small gaps cut into the walls and covered with wattle shutters, since glass—the product of beechwood ash fired in a charcoal furnace with washed sand—was a precious, and probably an imported, commodity.

A Life of Labor

Village communities provided reassuringly constant backdrops for a life. The average Anglo-Saxon could probably recognise every duck, chicken, and pig in his village and knew whom it belonged to—as he knew everything about his neighbours' lives. His social circle would not have filled three or four pages in a modern Filofax, and he would never have needed fresh leaves for updating, since the parents of his neighbours had been his parents' neighbours, and their children were destined to live their lives side-by-side with his. How else could life be? The closest modern parallel is with the restricted and repetitious circle of friends that surround the central families of radio and television soap-opera characters. In the year 1000, the same Christian names were often passed down traditionally inside families, but there were no surnames. There was not yet any need for them.

In the countryside around the villages, the fields were beginning to take on a shape that we would recognise, thanks to the labours of the ploughman with his powerful but cumbersome train of oxen. They cut the soil deep and long, but they were awkward to turn when the end of the furrow had been reached. So just as the village livestock grazed together on communal pasture, the fields created for arable cultivation were also organised on a community basis, with each unit of ploughland taking the form of a long and comparatively narrow strip.

Aelfric, the Cerne Abbas schoolteacher [taught from 987 to 1002], got his pupils to practice their Latin by learning a dialogue in which the pupils played the parts of different farm labourers, describing their work to a master who cross-questioned them:

Master What do you say, ploughman? How do you carry out your work?

"Ploughman"	Oh, I work very hard, dear lord. I go out at daybreak driving the oxen to the field, and yoke them to the plough; for fear of my lord, there is no winter so severe that I dare hide at home; but the oxen having been yoked and the share and coulter fastened to the plough, I must plough a full acre or more every day.
Master	Have you any companion?
"Ploughman"	I have a lad driving the oxen with a goad, who is now also hoarse because of the cold and shouting.
Master	What else do you do in the day?
"Ploughman"	I do more than that, certainly. I have to fill the oxen's bins with hay, and water them, and carry their muck outside.
Master	Oh, oh! It's hard work.
"Ploughman"	It's hard work, sir, because I am not free.

Beholden to the Lord of the Manor

The ploughman's colloquy draws attention to the basic and unromantic reality of English life in the year 1000—the reliance on slave labour. In 1066 the Normans were to bring to England their military-based arrangement of landholding known to generations of school children as the feudal system, with the hierarchy of serfs, villeins, and lords whose niceties are much argued over by historians. But prior to 1066, virtually all the documentary sources—wills, land deeds, and the literature of the day—clearly show that the basic underpinning of the rural economy in several parts of England was a class of workers who can only be described as slaves.

It is a commonplace that slavery made up the basis of life in the classical world, but it is sometimes assumed that slavery came to an end with the fall of Rome. In fact, the Germanic tribes who conquered Rome captured, kept, and traded in slaves as energetically as the Romans did—as indeed did the Arab conquerors of the Mediterranean. The purpose of war from the fifth to the tenth centuries was as much to capture bodies as it was to capture land, and the tribes of central Germany enjoyed particular success raiding their Slavic neighbours. If you purchased a bondservant in

Europe in the centuries leading up to the year 1000, the chances were that he or she was a "Slav"—hence the word "slave."

In England, the Anglo-Saxons proved to be slavers on a par with their Germanic cousins. *Weallas,* or Welshman, was one of the Old English words for slave—which showed where the Anglo-Saxons got their slaves. When, in 1086 A.D., the Normans commissioned their Domesday survey of the land they had conquered, it showed that there were significantly more slaves in the west of England than in the east, reflecting the closeness of Wales, and also the fact that Bristol was a slave port, trading with the Viking merchants based in Ireland. According to contemporary chronicles, eleventh-century Dublin operated the largest slave market in western Europe.

But war was not the only source of slaves. Anglo-Saxon law codes cited "slavery" as the penalty for offences ranging from certain types of theft to incest. In this latter case, the male involved became a slave of the king, while the woman was consigned to the service of the local bishop. Execution was evidently considered too severe a penalty for such an offence, while long-term imprisonment was not a practical possibility. Prisons did not develop until stone buildings and iron bars made them feasible, and since impoverished offenders had no money to pay fines, the only thing they could forfeit was their labour.

People also surrendered themselves into bondage at times of famine or distress, when they simply could not provide for their families any more. In later centuries there was the poorhouse or the bankruptcy law to help cope with such tragedies, but in the year 1000 the starving man had no other resort but to kneel before his lord or lady and place his head in their hands. No legal document was involved, and the new bondsman would be handed a bill-hook or ox-goad in token of his fresh start in servitude. It was a basic transaction—heads for food. The original old English meaning of lord was "loaf-giver," and Geatfleda, a lady of Northumbria, made the transaction explicit in the will she drew up in the 990s: "for the love of God and for the need of her soul, [Geatfleda] has given freedom to Ecceard, the blacksmith, and Aelfstan and his wife and all their offspring, born and unborn, and Arcil and Cole and Ecgferth [and] Ealdhun's daughter, and all those people whose heads she took for their food in the evil days."

Slavery still exists today in a few corners of the world, and from the security of our own freedom, we find the concept degrading and inhuman. But in the year 1000 very few people were free in the sense that we understand the word today. Almost everyone was beholden to someone more powerful than themselves, and the men and women who had surrendered themselves into bondage lived in conditions that were little different to those of any other member of the labouring classes. "Slave" is the only way to describe their servitude, but we should not envisage them manacled like a galley slave in ancient times, or living in segregated barracks like eighteenth-century slaves on the cotton plantations—or, indeed, like the workers in South African mines in our own times. Most bondsmen lived in what we would now describe as "tied" accommodation in a village with their families, and probably reared their own livestock as well. They were the men with the spades.

In the year 1000 people could not imagine themselves without a protector. You had a lord in heaven and you needed a lord on earth. The ploughman in Aelfric's *Colloquy* talked resentfully about his fear of his lord, and the fact that he worked so hard because his master required it. But other medieval documents proposed faithful service to a good master as a considerable—even a life-fulfilling—source of satisfaction, as it was for many servants right into our own times. It is a late twentieth-century innovation to scorn the concept of "service." In the year 1000 every English village had its local lord who provided an umbrella of protection for his neighbourhood, and that relationship involved a significant element of mutual respect. Anglo-Saxon lords never exercised, or attempted to claim, the notorious *droit de seigneur* whereby manorial law in some parts of Europe gave the local lord the right to bed the young brides of the village on their wedding night, and there were significant limits on their powers.

Medieval Knighthood

Hans-Werner Goetz

The knight in armor is one of the dominant images of the Middle Ages. Knighthood emerged during the ninth and tenth centuries as a separate social class in European society. Knights were above the peasantry, but because of their humble heritage and lack of funds, knights were far below the nobility for whom they worked. The dawn of the Crusades gave the knights prestige and changed their social status within European society. Knights acquired land by pledging military protection to the landowner. The acquisition of land elevated the knight from common soldier to aristocrat.

By the thirteenth century, the concept of knighthood changed entirely. The ideal knight was viewed as a protector of the weak and the defender of Christian faith. He was required to live by a strict moral code and be devoted to his lord.

Professor Hans-Werner Goetz teaches late ancient and medieval history at Ruhr University and has published several books and articles on conceptual history and peasant history. In this selection, Goetz outlines the duties and obligations for the medieval knight in European society. Throughout the medieval period, those duties and obligations proved to be too rigorous for most men to follow; therefore, those who were able to adhere to the strict moral and social code were revered by the whole of society up to the late Middle Ages. By the end of the Middle Ages, new military strategies and weapons made the knight less important in warfare. Knights formed new, nonmilitary orders where tournaments and jousting were offered for entertainment to the citizenry.

The institution of knighthood was a European phenomenon. Originating in southern France, it spread northward before fanning out via Flanders and Burgundy into the western regions of the German Empire, flourishing between 1100 and 1250.

Hans-Werner Goetz, *Life in the Middle Ages: From the Seventh to the Thirteenth Century,* edited by Steven Rowan and translated by Albert Wimmer. Notre Dame, IN: University of Notre Dame Press, 1993.

While our overall historical picture of knighthood is for the most part quite clear, it nevertheless remains a constant source of discussion among scholars. Let us therefore present the institution of knighthood as the primary representative of courtly life in light of the current state of research.

The origins of knighthood go back to a military system. Knights (*Ritter*, horsemen) were armed warriors on horseback. Two terms were commonly used in Latin to express the same idea: *caballarius* (which gave rise to French *chevalier*, Spanish *caballero*, and Italian *cavaliere*) [all meaning horseman] and the more commonly used Latin term *miles* (which referred in its basic meaning to simply a warrior, but was increasingly restricted to mean only "knight"). The narrowing of this concept stems from changes in the military structure during the eighth and ninth centuries. While an army consisting of foot soldiers had been recruited from the ranks of free men during Carolingian [under the rule of Charlemagne] times, elite military units were now formed with heavily armed horsemen on battle steeds which they had bred and trained themselves. This required constant training, so that one may speak—perhaps not entirely correctly—of a "professional warrior." However, the professional dimension of knighthood was considerably more complicated. It was, for example, certainly expensive to be a mounted warrior; by the eighth century, the value of both horse and equipment approximated that of forty-five cows or fifteen breeding mares, and by the eleventh century it already approached the value of five to ten oxen. Since a certain degree of wealth was a prerequisite for knighthood, knights were largely identical with landowners or—since they did not cultivate any land themselves—with secular manorial lords. Land-ownership existed in different forms, and private ownership (next to the Crown and Church) was primarily in the hands of the nobility. But the economic basis for land ownership was also in the form of a fief [a fee or grant usually in land] bestowed by the king, an ecclesiastical lord, a higher-ranking secular nobleman or officeholder. Thus, in addition to the nobility, knighthood consisted of the royal vassals, ecclesiastical vassals and vassals of the high nobility who were pledged to serve (*servitium*), primarily in the military. The military structure of the high Middle Ages was built entirely on a tiered feudal system with vassals and subvassals. As a result, various functions were discharged by knights who, as a group, were also manorial lords, warriors, and vassals, exhibiting a life-style commensurate with their position in society. . . .

Becoming a Knight

The social boundaries of knighthood were also visibly formalized, making knighthood in effect a "career." Sons of vassals were sent to be taught the art of knighthood at about the age of ten to twelve, or to serve as weapons-bearers at the court of a lord. At approximately the age of fourteen, they were referred to as *Junker* (= *Jungherr*, squires), serving as attendants to a knight. They could become knights by the age of twenty, although not everybody reached this level. By the eleventh century, official recognition as a knight required special induction (first attested for kings and sons of kings), the ceremony of knighting by which a knight became a *miles factus*.

Dubbing (*dubbatio*), a blow by hand or sword on the nape or with the flat of a blade on the left shoulder, was an act with which we connect knighting today; it also represented the final stage in a long development. It is found in France by the twelfth century, although it did not become customary in Germany until the fourteenth century. Handing over arms had originally been central to a ceremony performed by solemnly girding the sword (*cingere aliquem cingulo militaris*), the *Schwertleite*, a ritual in turn embedded in a series of ceremonial acts largely borrowed from the royal anointing ceremony. . . .

According to the characterization already made, wars and battles became the principle activities for knights (though not their only one). The armored war horses (*dextrarius*) which knights took into battle (and mounted only during actual battles), together with their marching horse (*palefridus*) and one pack-horse, became an object of affectionate description particularly in German literature. . . .

Such a war horse was armored and later often decorated with a colorful or embroidered caparison. Originally, a knight protected himself in battle with a knee-length, shortsleeve (later footlength and long-sleeved) chain mail shirt equipped even with gloves and a cowl. This outfit was made of interwoven, riveted metal links. Underneath it he wore a fabric shirt (a *Wams* or doublet that originally protruded) to protect his skin. Sometimes—in France since the middle of the twelfth century—following eastern custom, knights also donned a tunic (*Waffenrock*) over their coat of mail. Seignorial ostentatiousness displaced functional clothing. By the thirteenth century there was a tendency to cloak both rider and horse completely. The helmet consisted of a skullcap (*Glocke*), and the facial plate was replaced by a casque (*Topfhelm*) with slits (called "windows"). For purposes of easy identification by either friend or foe, distinctive external markings became necessary in the form of a crest and a coat of arms. (The earliest evidence is the *planta genista* branch on Godfrey of Anjou's tomb at Le Mans from 1149.) Pennants attached to lances were also helpful. Among the protective weapons were shields, which tended to become smaller as time went on, as a result of complete armament. Also, stirrups were most important both as a prerequisite for heavy armament and for a new form of doing battle by raising oneself up. . . . Sword and spear were traditional attack weapons, as well as a tilting lance which measured at least three meters and weighed from two to five kilograms. While riding, the knight carried it vertically, supported by a bracket, and aimed it horizontally at an enemy during an attack. Considering the weight of these armaments, a knight required one or even several attendants (a page and possibly some squires), constituting the basic military unit. . . .

Knightly Ideals and Reality

Knights were constantly forced to prove their knightliness (their *werdekeit,* worthiness) by demonstrating through bravery as well as conduct the qualities of *ere* (honor), *triuwe* (loyalty), *reht* (justice), *milde* (generosity), and especially *mâze* (a sense of balance). Interesting and even seemingly realistic (because they stem from the early period of knighthood) are the king's exhortations given to Ruodlieb (a knight in a German epic poem) upon the latter's return home. . . ; when he says, "Even if your road is covered with mud / extending broadly throughout the village / you must not let your horse leave the path / and ride through planted fields." (This warning is reminiscent of the protection granted to peasants in conjunction with the various peace agreements, although the king hardly finishes on a flattering note when he says, "lest the peasant maltreat you and take away your horse.") In matters of love, according to the king, class distinctions were to be observed . . . :

> Never treat your own maidservant, / no matter how beautiful, / as your equal, / as if she were a marriageable woman! / [The reason being:] she will rebel / against you / and refuse to show you respect; / for she will certainly believe / that she must now appear as lady of the house; / once she becomes your sweetheart / and sits down at your table / after lying next to you in bed / and eating at your table, / she will always want to lord it over / everything. / All this will bring a good man / dishonor.

Thus the king's advice is rather practical, clearly influenced by contemporary views. Concerning marriage the following is said . . . :

> Should you wish someday / to court a truly fine woman / in order to raise children with her, / one that you will want to embrace gladly, / then look for a wife / in a respectable house / and only if your mother / will have no objections against her! / Once you have chosen her in this fashion, / be sure to afford her every bit of honor. / Be gentle and treat her well, / but always remain her lord / so that she may never become contrary / and start arguing with you! / For there is no greater shame / for a husband / than being obedient to the one / whose rightful lord he is supposed to be.

Thus, the highly touted "courtly love" had its practical limitations, and knightly society remained male-dominated. . . .

These rather practical admonitions offered by the king to Ruodlieb illustrate that ethical conduct could easily be tantamount to personal well-being; at the same time, they warn against equating the highly stylized ideal of knighthood found in the later courtly epics with reality. However, this ethical bond provided knighthood with a new, basically timeless sense of worthiness.

Medieval Women at Work

Eileen Power

In the early Middle Ages (A.D. 500–A.D. 1100), two social classes existed: the nobility and the peasants. Peasant women knew only a life of hard labor. For the most part, peasants were oppressed during the Middle Ages regardless of gender. Women of nobility, however, enjoyed an array of powers and rights. They were able to inherit lands, manage landed estates, and open and run religious homes. After the early Middle Ages the rights and liberties of noblewomen slowly deteriorated as the church grew in power and influence. By the twelfth and thirteenth centuries, the noblewoman's position in society had waned. One reason for the deterioration was the church's perception of women: Women were temptresses (Eve in the Garden of Eden) and mothers (the Virgin Mary). This dichotomy aided in severely curtailing the rights of the noblewoman.

While the female nobility witnessed the erosion of their rights (women could not attend schools, go into politics, or practice medicine), lower-class women saw an improvement of their rights. With the emergence of the city, the middle class was born. Middle-class women found themselves in the unique position of earning income apart from their husbands. They owned businesses, dominated the silk weaving trade, and worked in trades such as brewing, cultivating the land, and copper mining. Many husbands and wives worked together in shops, and a wife could run her husband's business upon his death. In 1363, England allowed women to have more than one trade, whereas men were only allowed one.

The following selection, written by medieval historian Eileen Power, profiles the medieval woman during the late Middle Ages. Power, a popular lecturer on medieval history, explores the medieval working woman's integral role in society.

At the close of the Middle Ages, middle-class women enjoyed

Eileen Power, *Medieval Women*, edited by M.M. Postan. New York: Cambridge University Press, 1975.

a measure of economic success; however, noblewomen were confined to running the household and doing needlework. Not until the early modern era did noblewomen see a return to the rights they once enjoyed in the early Middle Ages.

In considering the typical lady of the manor and the typical housewife of the well-to-do bourgeoisie, full account had to be taken of women's work in the home. Both among the gentry and among the bourgeoisie women did a great deal in their homes and their homes gave them great scope. The wife also had to understand her husband's job so as to take his place in his absence. The emphasis changes somewhat as we pass from the home to the labour market, from the gentry and the bourgeoisie to the working woman in town and country. As we descend the social scale, we do not find the role of women declining. On the contrary her activity, if she is alone, her importance in the life of the family, if she is married, is all the greater for the modesty, indeed exigency, of her income and possessions. In the more exalted affairs of society, the military, the diplomatic, the political, the professional, women (save on exceptional occasions) influenced events comparatively little; but they played an equal part with men in the economic life of nations. Like men, they were driven to offer themselves for hire, or otherwise to work for their living.

The appearance of women in the labour market in the Middle Ages was due to the same reason as their work today, viz. it was necessary for the married woman to earn a supplementary wage and necessary for the single woman to earn a livelihood. In every class of western society marriage is a career, to which most girls aspire. But in the Middle Ages, and often today, marriage by no means always meant that a woman devoted herself to the home and was exempt from some industry. As we shall see presently the wife of a craftsman almost always worked as her husband's assistant in his trade, or if not, she often eked out the family income by some such bye industry as brewing and spinning; sometimes she even practised a separate trade as a *femme sole.*

Moreover, not all women could hope to marry. For a variety of reasons the total number of women, then as now, was in excess of the number of men. This was due to the greater difficulty of rearing boys and possibly to the greater mortality among men in the perennial plagues of the Middle Ages; partly also to the greater risk of sudden death which they ran in wars, or town feuds, or general disturbances of the countryside; and partly to the celibacy of the large body of monks and still larger body of secular clergy whose numbers were very much greater than those of nuns. . . .

Assisting Their Husbands

It may be that large numbers of women were to be found in the same occupation which before the first war provided the main employment for women, especially the unmarried ones, that is domestic service. Yet it is by no means true (as sometimes stated) that women in the Middle Ages were, as a rule, unpaid domestic workers and not wage earners. The cases in which a man was helped by his wife and daughter and perhaps maidservant in his trade were perhaps more numerous than the cases of women who carried on an independent occupation. Even gild regulations, which expressly exclude women from participation in a trade, regarded this unprofessional labour as a matter of course and made exceptions for wives and daughters. In 1372 when articles were drawn up for the leathersellers and pouch-makers of London and for dyers serving these trades, wives of dyers of leather were sworn together with their husbands to do their calling. At a time when factories were unknown and industries were carried on by craftsmen in their own homes and workshops, it was natural they should invoke the assistance of wives as well as that of apprentices and journeymen.

The fact that wives were accustomed to assist husbands in crafts is perhaps the reason why all through the later Middle Ages we find large numbers of widows carrying on their dead husbands' trade. Sometimes gild regulations specifically allow them to do so. Husbands often expected wives to carry on business after their death, for we frequently find men providing in their wills that their apprentices should serve out their term with their widows, or for leaving to their wives implements belonging to trade.

Trades thus carried on by widows ranged from that of merchants on a large scale, trafficking in ships and dealing with the

Crown, to that of small craftsmen. No small amount of knowledge and ability was required to manage a large and important business; and widows doing so must have been competent folk, well able to hold their own even in the complications of foreign commerce. . . .

Careers for the Medieval Woman

It must not be supposed, however, that women's work in the labour market in the Middle Ages was confined to assisting their husbands while they were alive or carrying on their husbands' business after their death. Many unmarried women supported themselves as shopkeepers and wage earners and many married women carried on occupations of their own perfectly distinct from those of their husbands.

Girls were often apprenticed to trades in the same way as boys. The Statute of 1407 which tried (in the interest of agriculture) to confine industry to men and women possessing annual rents to twenty shillings per annum, forbade those who had not this amount to apprentice a child to a trade; and the statute specifically speaks of 'son or daughter'. Wills of London citizens often leave provision for daughters as well as sons to be apprenticed. Where a gentleman of the upper class will leave a sum of money to his daughter as a dowry to wed her or to put her into a nunnery, a father in an urban occupation will leave money to wed her or put her to a trade.

Sometimes girls, as well as boys, were sent out at a very early age to work, for exploitation of child labour was by no means an invention of the Industrial Revolution. Very small children helped mothers to sort and card wool for spinning in their own homes. . . .

Women thus apprenticed could support themselves by their craft if they remained unmarried, or *femmes soles* as they were designated. But it is an interesting fact that there were not only many single women thus engaged in trade, but that many married women went on with their own jobs after marriage and carried on a trade separate from their husbands. Regulations of many medieval towns provide for treatment of wife as a single woman in such cases. When she becomes involved in a trade dispute she is not 'covered' by her husband, i.e. he cannot be made responsible for her debts as he would otherwise be. This was for example the Lincoln rule:

> If any woman that has a husband use any craft within the city, whereof her husband meddles not, she shall be charged as a sole woman as touching such things as belongeth to her craft. And if a plaint be taken against such a woman, she shall answer and plead as a sole woman and make her law and take other advantage in court by plea or otherwise for her discharge. And if she be condemned she shall be committed to prison till she be agreed with the plaintiff, and on goods or chattels that belongeth to husb. shall be confiscated.

We find similar rules in London and a large number of other towns. They were intended for the protection of husbands but none the less represented a notable advance in the position of married women under the common law.

Occupations for the Medieval Woman

Medieval industry was open to women and they played a by no means inconsiderable part in it. There was hardly a craft in which we do not find women. They were butchers, chandlers, iron-mongers, net-makers, shoe-makers, glovers, girdlers, haber-dashers, purse-makers, cap-makers, skinners, bookbinders, gilders, painters, silk-weavers and embroiderers, spicers, smiths and goldsmiths among many other trades.

This spread of occupations in which women were engaged raises an interesting question. What was the attitude of men towards the co-operation or competition of female labour; and what in particular was the position occupied by women in the predominantly male craft gilds?

We have seen men working side by side with women in many industries, but there are traces of jealousy of the competition of female labour (other than that of the wife or daughter of a crafts-man). Thus the London Girdlers enacted in 1344 that no man of the trade should set any woman to work other than his wife or daughter. The Lincoln Fullers ordered in 1297 that 'no one of craft shall work at wooden bar with a woman unless with wife of master or her handmaid'. A complaint made at Bristol in 1461 that weavers set to work or hired to others their wives, daugh-ters and maidens, 'by the which many & divers of the King's liege people, likely men to do the king service in his wars and defence of this land and sufficiently learned in the said craft goeth vagrant and unoccupied and may not have their labour to their living', and weavers were forbidden to employ women except those then getting their livelihood thus.

The reason occasionally given for barring employment of women was that work of a particular craft was too hard for them, but the main reason was the same as that which animates hostility to female labour today. Women's wages were lower even for the same work, and men were afraid of being undercut by cheap labour. . . .

Brewing and Bread-Making

It has already been mentioned here that women also took part in large numbers of trades connected with making and purveying of food. Brewing, for instance, was largely, though not exclusively, in the hands of women and was a favourite occupation for married women. Information about them is chiefly obtained from records of continual breach of the Assize of Ale. It is rare to find a record of any session of a borough or manor court in which brewsters were not fined for using false measures or for buying and selling contrary to assize. In the last years of the fourteenth century large numbers of brewsters were prosecuted under the Statute of Labourers for demanding excessive payment.

Bread-making was also an occupation carried on by women, although it seems in most cases to have been men's work. It was largely a town craft: in London and other large towns bakeresses or baxters were very numerous. Like brewsters they sold their wares either retail or wholesale, and like them they were often prosecuted under the Assize of Bread and Ale. And it is not uncommon to find a woman doubling the two crafts.

Among trades followed by women there was a number of other occupations, e.g. selling in markets, which from the fact they had no connection with gilds were regarded essentially as women's occupations. Regraters or hucksters (i.e. retailers) were often women. They sold bread, ale, fish, poultry and all manner of eatables. We find a Nottingham jury presenting that all hucksters of Nottingham sold garlic, flour, salt, tallow candles, butter,

In addition to managing household duties, peasant women worked the land, spending hours doing strenuous labor in the fields.

cheeses and suchlike commodities very dearly and that all of them made candles without wicks to the deception of the people. . . .

A Life of Hard Work

Much less prominent in medieval sources, perhaps because it was taken for granted, was the largest class of working women, peasants and dwellers on all manors scattered up and down England. Most of them were expected, if they were married, to share in all their husband's labours on their family holdings. In addition they were burdened with chores which were traditionally feminine. The keeping of the house was of course one of them, the making of cloths and clothes (both for own use and for sale) was another. When Helmbrecht, an ambitious peasant hero of the famous German poem of the same name, tries to persuade his sister Gotelinde to flee the house of her peasant parents and marry a man who would enable her to lead the life of a lady, he reminds her of what her existence would otherwise be. 'You will never be more wretched than if you marry a peasant. You will be compelled to spin, to scour the flax, to combe the hemp, wash and wring clothes, dig up the beets.' Heimbrecht's list of the tasks which life imposed on a peasant wife was of course too short. For instance, it says nothing of the strenuous hours and weeks which a working wife was called upon to spend by her husband's side in fields and pastures.

These tasks weighed no less, often even more, on women who, whether married or not, possessed holdings in their own names—mostly widows, or unmarried women. This was perhaps the most hardworked class of all. In every manorial survey one will find a certain number of women as free tenants, villeins or cotters, holding their virgate of few acres like men and liable to pay the same services for them—so many days' labour a week perhaps, so many boon services at sowing or harvest, so many cartings, so many eggs or pullets or pence per year. No doubt they hired men for heavy ploughing but probably performed other services in person.

We find in manorial accounts women hired by the bailiff to do all sorts of agricultural labour. In fact there was hardly any work except ploughing for which they were not engaged, e.g. planting peas and beans, weeding, reaping, binding, threshing, winnowing, thatching. They did much of the sheep shearing. One of the most important of regular servants of the manor was the dairy woman or *daye* who looked after dairy and poultry on the manor farm. . . .

Such compensations as this life had—and it had some—were not all manorial. The village society was advancing steadily in freedom in Western Europe during the Middle Ages, and harsh and coarse and laborious as it was, peasant women's life had its rude gaieties and there may often have been some truth in Christine de Pisan's [a medieval artist and writer] judgment: 'Albeit they be fed with coarse bread, milk, lard and pottage and drink water, and albeit they have care and labour enow, yet is their life surer, yea, they have greater sufficiency, than some that be of high estate.' Christine could with some justice have added greater equality and perhaps even greater self-respect to the compensating advantages of the peasant woman's existence.

The Christian Church at Work

Robert Bartlett

Throughout the Middle Ages, the church was the most centralized and absolute institution in Europe. The church and its teachings permeated daily life. The events of birth, marriage, and death made the church the center of activity for the medieval village, town, and castle. The church was the center of social life for the medieval village; all festivals and holidays were religious. The church also provided services for the poor; built hospitals, bridges, and roads; established institutes of learning; outlined moral instruction for daily living; and provided spiritual stability to the populace. In the following excerpt author and editor Robert Bartlett discusses the tremendous impact the church had on daily life during the Middle Ages. Bartlett is Wardlaw Professor of Medieval History at the University of St. Andrews, Scotland.

The Term 'The Church' usually conjures up images of a specifically clerical or monastic community, from the pope to the parish priest, from cardinals and inquisitors to simple monks, friars and nuns. In the Middle Ages the word could also be used in a broader sense. The simplest and most direct translation of the word 'society' in medieval Europe would be 'the Church'. Everybody apart from the tiny Jewish and Muslim minorities would be baptized. Their marriage and burial would also usually take place under the auspices of the clergy. 'Christian' was the label that all these people, from whatever region—Bavaria, Scotland, Connacht, Sicily—could apply to themselves. Of course there were ethnic and class identities, but over them all was the fact that these scattered populations saw themselves as part of a larger Christendom.

Amongst this Christian population some had undertaken a more complete commitment to the religious life. Priests, deacons

---

Robert Bartlett, *Medieval Panorama*. Los Angeles: J. Paul Getty Museum, 2001.

and other clerics promised chastity and bore the external marks of the tonsure and clerical dress, while those who entered the monastic orders abandoned not only sexual and family life but also private property and their own will. The idea of Christian monasticism, that is, of communities living a life of chastity and poverty in obedience to a superior, arose in the deserts of Egypt in the late Roman period, spread to Western Europe and there was given its distinctive Western form by St Benedict of Nursia in the sixth century. His *Rule*, the foundation stone of Benedictine monasticism, was the basic code of almost all western monasteries by the year 1000.

The Life of the Religious Orders

The life of a Benedictine monk or nun centred on the cycle of church services. The prayers, chants and psalms of the Divine Office and the celebration of Mass required hours each day, from dawn to night. The year was shaped by the liturgical rhythm, with its high points at Easter, Christmas and Pentecost. At least a basic literacy was necessary for these activities and, in the early Middle Ages, the production and preservation of books was almost exclusively the work of the monasteries. Since many monks and nuns entered the monastery as children and were bound by a vow of stability to remain there, it was possible for them to spend virtually their entire lives within one community—'a cloistered life' in the literal sense.

By the eleventh century the Benedictine monasteries of Western Europe had become rich, profiting from the willingness of kings and great aristocrats to give them lands in return for their prayers. The liturgy became ever more elaborate. Abbots of the greater monasteries, such as Cluny in Burgundy, the most famous abbey of its time, were figures of international importance. It is not surprising that this provoked a reaction, or movement of reform, as its protagonists viewed it. The monastic life, they argued, was meant to be simpler and more austere. Monks should work with their hands and not be landlords. The elaborate decoration and carvings of the old Benedictine churches were distracting. 'Back to the desert' was the watchword of the reformers.

The Cistercians were the most successful of the reformed Benedictines. Founded at Cîteaux (not far from Cluny) in 1098, the order numbered over 500 abbeys by the year 1200, in large part because of the charismatic leadership of St Bernard of Clairvaux, who, although in rank only an abbot, became a dominating figure in the ecclesiastical politics of the years between the 1120s and his death in 1153. He encouraged the crusading movement, assailed those whom he suspected of heresy, and preached and wrote with passion and eloquence of the mystical path to God. Everywhere Cistercian monasteries sprang up, marked by their simple, uniform plan, their austerity of style and the fact that, initially at least, their lands were worked by monks and lay brothers rather than by peasant tenants.

The Christian Life

The Cistercians, and other reformed orders of the twelfth century, while representing a new adaptation of the ancient tradition of Christian monasticism, still preserved many of its established features. The friars of the early thirteenth century were more revolutionary in their basic approach to the full-time religious vocation. The model of St Francis, the founder and inspiration of the friars, pointed to a life of wandering, preaching and begging from door to door (hence the friars are also termed 'mendicants' or beggars). Just as the Cistercians had aroused the religious enthusiasm of Europe in the twelfth century, so the Franciscans and Dominicans dominated the thirteenth, establishing themselves across the whole of Catholic Christendom, forming an intellectual elite that elaborated a Christian form of philosophy ('scholasticism') and through their preaching bringing Christian doctrine and practice to the laity in a way never before attempted.

Over the course of its long history the Christian religion has often veered between stressing belief in a set of doctrines and concentrating on rituals and practices. Medieval Christianity was certainly based on a set of doctrines, and those who dissented from those doctrines were persecuted and sometimes executed, but the heart of the religion was not creed but a range of ritual and devotional customs. The Christian life was framed by the sacraments of baptism, confirmation, marriage and anointing of the dead, and found regular expression in the sacraments of mass and penance. The fate of the soul after death could be affected by the prayers and charity of the living. Good deeds, such as alms-giving, brought merit. So did punishment of the flesh: fasting and flagellation were ways of lessening the future pains of purgatory by inflicting them here and now.

The Christian could seek the aid of supernatural power in many ways, from the saints, from the angels, from Mary, mother of God, and from Christ himself, as the baby in his mother's arms, as the tortured figure on the crucifix or in the form of the Eucharist, which was viewed as Christ's body and had, from 1264, its own annual feast day, Corpus Christi ('the body of Christ'). The whole of Western Europe was filled with shrines where local saints could be invoked for help, especially for their healing powers. Some of these shrines became centres of international pilgrimage. Santiago de Compostela, where the bones of St James were supposedly discovered in the ninth century, drew pilgrims from all over Western Christendom and their route across northern Spain—'the French trail' as it was called—was marked by new bridges, hostels and churches, and towns flourishing from their traffic (its significance is illustrated by the fact that in modern Spanish the Milky Way is termed 'the Santiago trail').

Especially in the later Middle Ages, mystics and visionaries were important in the Christian religious life. The Low Countries and the Rhineland produced remarkable figures, including Meister Eckhart, his followers Johann Tauler and Heinrich Suso, and the Fleming, Jan van Ruysbroeck, whose *Adornment of the Spiritual Marriage* culminated in a lyrical account of the mystic's goal: 'rapturous meeting,' 'eternal rest in the fruitive embrace of an outpouring Love', 'the dark silence in which all lovers lose themselves'. Women had been important in Christian mysticism since the time of Hildegard of Bingen (d. 1179) and they continued to be so throughout the following centuries, with such figures as Catherine of Siena and the English mystics Juliana of Norwich and Margery Kempe pursuing ecstatic rapture and visionary experiences.

Challenges to the Church's Authority

The medieval Church was not a democratic or liberal institution but a hierarchical and authoritarian one. Those who dissented from official doctrine were not tolerated. Apart from in the exceptional case of the Jews (and Muslims in some parts of Spain), the Church authorities regarded difference in belief as an evil to be rooted out. Theologians had to be careful to avoid unorthodox theories or, like Peter Abelard in the twelfth century and John Wycliffe in the fourteenth, they might find themselves the target of accusations of heresy. Abelard's books were burned, but, as the poet Heine remarked, 'where they begin by burning books, they end by burning men'. As the Church came to feel that the challenge of heresy was growing in strength, so it devised more thorough and more brutal forms of inquisition and repression. The forcing house for these new policies was southern France, where the heretical groups known as Cathars became so numerous that Pope Innocent III launched a crusade against them in 1209, while in the 1230s Pope Gregory IX followed this up by establishing the inquisition to hunt out heretics.

Catharism was eventually exterminated, after hundreds of its followers had been burned, but other heretical movements arose, challenging the authority of the Church hierarchy and advocating alternative doctrines and structures. The Waldensians believed that ordinary lay people, including women, had the right to preach; the Spiritual Franciscans clashed with the papacy because of their extreme commitment to the ideal of poverty; the Lollards, who took up some of Wycliffe's ideas, cited Scripture to attack the authority and property of the Church, rejected pilgrimage, prayers to the dead and reverence for images and argued that every righteous layman was a true priest. The most successful of the heretical movements of the later Middle Ages was that of the Hussites, who actually seized control of Bohemia for seventeen years (1419–36), defeating crusading armies that were sent against them and threatening to spread their beliefs through force into the neighbouring territories. They had a radical and a moderate wing, the former advocating complete disendowment of the Church and socially revolutionary principles. Not unnaturally, the Hussites have been seen as precursors of the Reformation a century later that destroyed medieval Christendom for good.

Saint Benedict's Rule for Monasteries

Saint Benedict

Medieval parish priests and churchmen administered to the spiritual life of the medieval citizen. The priests and churchmen served their Christian congregations in the everyday world. However, many religious people desired to leave the material world and devote their life to praying and worshipping God. Numerous monasteries were built where monks and nuns could live and devote their lives to prayer, study, and benediction.

Monasteries required members to take a vow of poverty, chastity, and obedience for life. In addition to their vows, members agreed to live by an established rule or code of conduct. In the following excerpt Saint Benedict's rule for monasteries outlines what is expected from each monk. Saint Benedict was an Italian monk called Benedict of Nursia (480–547) who set up a monastery at Monte Cassino in Italy in about 529. His strict rule on monastic life became the basis of Roman Catholic monasticism.

When anyone is newly come for the reformation of his life, let him not be granted an easy entrance; but, as the Apostle says, "Test the spirits to see whether they are from God." If the newcomer, therefore, perseveres in his knocking, and if it is seen after four or five days that he bears patiently the harsh treatment offered him and the difficulty of admission, and that he persists in his petition, then let entrance be granted him, and let him stay in the guest house for a few days.

After that let him live in the novitiate, where the novices study, eat and sleep. A senior shall be assigned to them who is skilled in winning souls, to watch over them with the utmost care. Let him examine whether the novice is truly seeking God, and whether he is zealous for the Work of God, for obedience and for humiliations. Let the novice be told all the hard and

Saint Benedict, *St. Benedict's Rule for Monasteries*, translated by Leonard J. Doyle. Collegeville, MN: The Liturgical Press, 1948.

rugged ways by which the journey to God is made.

If he promises stability and perseverance, then at the end of two months let this Rule be read through to him, and let him be addressed thus: "Here is the law under which you wish to fight. If you can observe it, enter; if you cannot, you are free to depart." If he still stands firm, let him be taken to the above-mentioned novitiate and again tested in all patience. And after the lapse of six months let the Rule be read to him, that he may know on what he is entering. And if he still remains firm, after four months let the same Rule be read to him again.

A Life of Devotion to God

Then, having deliberated with himself, if he promises to keep it in its entirety and to observe everything that is commanded him, let him be received into the community. But let him understand that, according to the law of the Rule, from that day forward he may not leave the monastery nor withdraw his neck from under the yoke of the Rule which he was free to refuse or to accept during that prolonged deliberation.

He who is to be received shall make a promise before all in the oratory of his stability and of the reformation of his life and of obedience. This promise he shall make before God and His Saints, so that if he should ever act otherwise, he may know that he will be condemned by Him whom he mocks. Of this promise of his let him draw up a petition in the name of the Saints whose relics are there and of the Abbot who is present. Let him write this petition with his own hand; or if he is illiterate, let another write it at his request, and let the novice put his mark to it. Then let him place it with his own hand upon the altar; and when he has placed it there, let the novice at once intone this verse: "Receive me, O Lord, according to Your word, and I shall live: and let me not be confounded in my hope." Let the whole community answer this verse three times and add the "Glory be to the Father." Then let the novice brother prostrate himself at each one's feet, that they may pray for him. And from that day forward let him be counted as one of the community.

If he has any property, let him either give it beforehand to the poor or by solemn donation bestow it on the monastery, reserving nothing at all for himself, as indeed he knows that from that

Saint Benedict (pictured, center) outlined the code of conduct for monks. His strict rule became the foundation of monastic life.

day forward he will no longer have power even over his own body. At once, therefore, in the oratory, let him be divested of his own clothes which he is wearing and dressed in the clothes of the monastery. But let the clothes of which he was divested be put aside in the wardrobe and kept there. Then if he should ever listen to the persuasions of the devil and decide to leave the monastery (which God forbid), he may be divested of the monastic clothes and cast out. His petition, however, which the Abbot has taken from the altar, shall not be returned to him, but shall be kept in the monastery.

Offering One's Son to a Life of Religious Obedience

If anyone of the nobility offers his son to God in the monastery and the boy is very young, let his parents draw up the petition which we mentioned above; and at the oblation let them wrap the petition and the boy's hand in the altar cloth and so offer him.

As regards their property, they shall promise in the same petition under oath that they will never of themselves, or through an intermediary, or in any way whatever, give him anything or provide him with the opportunity of owning anything. Or else, if they are unwilling to do this, and if they want to offer something as an alms to the monastery for their advantage, let them make a donation of the property they wish to give to the monastery, reserving the income to themselves if they wish. And in this way let everything be barred, so that the boy may have no expectations whereby (which God forbid) he might be deceived and ruined, as we have learned by experience.

Let those who are less well-to-do make a similar offering. But those who have nothing at all shall simply draw up the petition and offer their son before witnesses at the oblation.

Priestly Entrance into the Monastery

If anyone of the priestly order should ask to be received into the monastery, permission shall not be granted him too readily. But if he is quite persistent in his resquest, let him know that he will have to observe the whole discipline of the Rule and that nothing will be relaxed in his favor, that it may be as it is written: "Friend, for what have you come?"

It shall be granted him, however, to stand next after the Abbot and to give blessings and to celebrate Mass, but only by order of the Abbot. Without such order let him not presume to do anything, knowing that he is subject to the discipline of the Rule; but rather let him give an example of humility to all.

If there happens to be question of an appointment or of some business in the monastery, let him expect the rank due him according to the date of his entrance into the monastery, and not the place granted him out of reverence for the priesthood.

If any clerics, moved by the same desire, should wish to join the monastery, let them be placed in a middle rank. But they too are to be admitted only if they promise observance of the Rule and their own stability.

Treatment of Guests

If a pilgrim monk coming from a distant region wants to live as a guest of the monastery, let him be received for as long a time as he desires, provided he is content with the customs of the place as he finds them and does not disturb the monastery by superfluous demands, but is simply content with what he finds. If, however, he censures or points out anything reasonably and with the humility of charity, let the Abbot consider prudently whether perhaps it was for that very purpose that the Lord sent him.

If afterwards he should want to bind himself to stability, his wish should not be denied him, especially since there has been opportunity during his stay as a guest to discover his character.

But if as a guest he was found exacting or prone to vice, not only should he be denied membership in the community, but he should even be politely requested to leave, lest others be corrupted by his evil life.

If, however, he has not proved to be the kind who deserves to be put out, he should not only on his own application be received as a member of the community, but he should even be persuaded to stay, that the others may be instructed by his example, and because in every place it is the same Lord who is served, the same King for whom the battle is fought.

Moreover, if the Abbot perceives that he is a worthy man, he may put him in a somewhat higher rank. And not only with regard to a monk but also with regard to those in priestly or clerical orders previously mentioned, the Abbot may establish them in a higher rank than would be theirs by date of entrance if he perceives that their life is deserving.

Let the Abbot take care, however, never to receive a monk from another known monastery as a member of his community without the consent of his Abbot or a letter of recommendation; for it is written, "Do not to another what you would not want done to yourself."

Trials and Tribulations

Chapter Preface

In early October 1347 twelve plague-bearing galley ships entered the port of Messina, Sicily. The diseased sailors had strange black swellings in their armpits and groins that oozed blood and pus and caused severe pain and ultimate death. The citizens, realizing too late that the sailors and their ships brought the pestilence, drove them out of the port, forcing them to find harbor elsewhere and thereby helping to spread the disease. The inhabitants sought to drive the danger away and, in doing so, helped plunge medieval Europe into one of the worst epidemics of bubonic plague in history.

The people of the Middle Ages were accustomed to famine, disease, violent death, and tragedy; however, the Black Death was unlike any other calamity they had experienced, and its psychological effects went deep. Its unknown cause (the connection between plague and rats was not understood until about the mid-1920s); its high mortality rate (about one-third of the population of Europe was killed by the plague); and its hideous physical manifestations (black blisters, swelling of the tongue, and subcutaneous hemorrhages) combined to make bubonic plague exceptionally terrifying. Many people believed the plague was visited upon them by an angry God. Physicians and learned men suggested causes that were erroneous (including inhalation of corrupted vapors in the air and misalignment of the moon and sun) and recommended remedies that were ineffectual at best (such as no bathing and no sleeping during the day). The plague was totally incomprehensible; the outbreak came on suddenly, killed all in its path, and could not be resisted. No form of defense—social, medical, or psychological—against an epidemic of its magnitude was present for the medieval person.

People's response to the plague was threefold: Some shut themselves off from the world and stayed in their homes, leading a sheltered, secluded life; some, believing that evil had befallen them and there was no way out, abandoned modesty and spent their days seeking pleasure in public places of entertainment; and some accepted their fate, spending their days living simply and comfortably. Nevertheless, the majority of people believed that the pestilence was a manifestation of God's wrath, so they looked to the clergy for help. Thousands descended on their parish churches, local monasteries, and cathedrals to ask for absolution for their sins and to do penance in the vain hope that this would abate the spread of the Black Death. Unfortunately, the disease continued to spread, and soon many clergy abandoned their posts and fled to the hills in hopes of escaping the inevitable death the disease brought.

Once the plague struck a certain area, towns, villages, and cities quickly succumbed to the pestilence. Extensive social and economic unrest sprang from the plague. Agriculture suffered from the lack of laborers; workers demanded higher wages; corruption among the clergy and government officials worsened; bands of people assaulted and robbed the afflicted or the dead; and family life was disrupted by family members' abandonment of those afflicted. Chaos on the social, moral, and economic levels reverberated throughout each class of society. The Black Death pervaded every aspect of medieval life.

Once the Black Death took hold and spread, it set Europe on a new path. The widespread deaths of landowners, serfs, craftsmen, and artisans created a large labor shortage in villages and towns throughout Europe. The working classes were now in a position to drive a hard bargain or to strike out on their own. The reduction of the population also liberated land for uses other than the cultivation of grains. Historians have viewed the plague as the stimulus for labor-saving technology; the origins of industrialization; the growth of nationalism; the increase in education and vernacular literature; the distrust of the clergy; and the genesis for the Reformation. By the end of the Middle Ages, the horror of the Black Death was just a mere memory, but the economic and social changes the pestilence caused had lingering effects well into the fifteenth century. The plague had forever changed the course of medieval Europe.

The Plague Delivers Death

Giovanni Boccaccio

In 1348 a plague struck and devastated most of Europe. The plague, commonly referred to as the Black Death, systematically spread from Sicily all the way to Sweden, killing most of those who contracted the deadly disease. For two long years the plague ravaged most of Europe, and when it was finished nearly three quarters of the population was dead. In the ensuing years, several outbreaks of the plague affected Europe, but not nearly as severely as the outbreak during 1348 through 1350. Giovanni Boccaccio (1323–1375) was an Italian poet and writer. In the following excerpt from his introduction to his collection of short stories entitled *The Decameron*, Boccaccio describes the horrors and decimation the plague brought to his native Florence, Italy. He details the physical symptoms of the Black Death and recounts the fear and viciousness that gripped his city and turned people against each other.

Let me say, then, that thirteen hundred and forty-eight years had already passed after the fruitful Incarnation of the Son of God when into the distinguished city of Florence, more noble than any other Italian city, there came a deadly pestilence. Either because of the influence of heavenly bodies or because of God's just wrath as a punishment to mortals for our wicked deeds, the pestilence, originating some years earlier in the East, killed an infinite number of people as it spread relentlessly from one place to another until finally it had stretched its miserable length all over the West. And against this pestilence no human wisdom or foresight was of any avail; quantities of filth were removed from the city by officials charged with the task; the entry of any sick person into the city was prohibited; and many directives were issued concerning the maintenance of good health.

Giovanni Boccaccio, *The Decameron*, translated by Mark Musa and Peter Bondanella. New York: New American Library, Inc., 1982.

Nor were the humble supplications rendered not once but many times by the pious to God, through public processions or by other means, in any way efficacious.

The Symptoms

Almost at the beginning of springtime of the year in question the plague began to show its sorrowful effects in an extraordinary manner. It did not assume the form it had in the East, where bleeding from the nose was a manifest sign of inevitable death, but rather it showed its first signs in men and women alike by means of swellings either in the groin or under the armpits, some of which grew to the size of an ordinary apple and others to the size of an egg (more or less), and the people called them *gavoccioli* (buboes). And from the two parts of the body already mentioned, in very little time, the said deadly *gavoccioli* began to spread indiscriminately over every part of the body; then, after this, the symptoms of the illness changed to black or livid spots appearing on the arms and thighs, and on every part of the body—sometimes there were large ones and other times a number of little ones scattered all around. And just as the *gavoccioli* were originally, and still are, a very definite indication of impending death, in like manner these spots came to mean the same thing for whoever contracted them. Neither a doctor's advice nor the strength of medicine could do anything to cure this illness; on the contrary, either the nature of the illness was such that it afforded no cure, or else the doctors were so ignorant that they did not recognize its cause and, as a result, could not prescribe the proper remedy (in fact, the number of doctors, other than the well-trained, was increased by a large number of men and women who had never had any medical training); at any rate, few of the sick were ever cured, and almost all died after the third day of the appearance of the previously described symptoms (some sooner, others later), and most of them died without fever or any other side effects.

A Very Contagious Disease

This pestilence was so powerful that it was transmitted to the healthy by contact with the sick, the way a fire close to dry or oily things will set them aflame. And the evil of the plague went even further: not only did talking to or being around the sick bring infection and a common death, but also touching the clothes of the sick or anything touched or used by them seemed to communicate this very disease to the person involved. What I am about to say is incredible to hear, and if I and others had not witnessed it with our own eyes, I should not dare believe it (let alone write about it), no matter how trustworthy a person I might have heard it from. Let me say, then, that the plague described here was of such virulence in spreading from one person to another that not only did it pass from one man to the next, but, what's more, it was often transmitted from the garments of a sick or dead man to animals that not only became contaminated by the disease but also died within a brief period of time. My own eyes, as I said earlier, were witness to such a thing one day: when the rags of a poor man who died of this disease were thrown into the public street, two pigs came upon them, and, as they are wont to do, first with their snouts and then with their teeth they took the rags and shook them around; and within a short time, after a number of convulsions, both pigs fell dead upon the ill-fated rags, as if they had been poisoned. From these and many similar or worse occurrences there came about such fear and such fantastic notions among those who remained alive that almost all of them took a very cruel attitude in the matter; that is, they completely avoided the sick and their possessions, and in so doing, each one believed that he was protecting his own good health.

Reacting to the Pestilence

There were some people who thought that living moderately and avoiding any excess might help a great deal in resisting this disease, and so they gathered in small groups and lived entirely apart from everyone else. They shut themselves up in those houses where there were no sick people and where one could live well by eating the most delicate of foods and drinking the finest of wines (doing so always in moderation), allowing no one to speak about or listen to anything said about the sick and the dead outside; these people lived, entertaining themselves with music and other pleasures that they could arrange. Others thought the opposite: they believed that drinking excessively, enjoying life, going about singing and celebrating, satisfying in every way the appetites as best one could, laughing, and making light of everything that happened was the best medicine for such a disease; so they practiced to the fullest what they believed by going from one tavern to another all day and night, drinking to excess; and they would often make merry in private homes, doing everything that pleased or amused them the most. This they were able to do easily, for everyone felt he was doomed to die and, as a result, abandoned his property, so that most of the houses had become common property, and any stranger who came upon them used them as if he were their rightful owner. In addition to this bestial behavior, they always managed to avoid the sick as best they could. And in this great affliction and misery of our city the revered authority of the laws, both divine and human, had fallen and almost completely disappeared, for, like other men, the ministers and executors of the laws were either dead or sick or so short of help that it was impossible for them to fulfill their duties; as a result, everybody was free to do as he pleased.

Many others adopted a middle course between the two attitudes just described: neither did they restrict their food or drink

A Plague Survivor's Tips on Staying Healthy

Tommaso del Garbo, an Italian citizen who survived the plague, offers a hygienic practice that remained standard for centuries.

Notaries, confessors, relations and doctors who visit the plague victims on entering their houses should open the windows so that the air is renewed [i.e. the corrupt air], and wash their hands with vinegar and rose water and also their faces, especially around their mouth and nostrils. It is also a good idea before entering the room to place in your mouth several cloves and eat two slices of bread soaked in the best wine and then drink the rest of the wine. Then when leaving the room you should douse yourself and your pulses with vinegar and rose water and touch your nose frequently with a sponge soaked in vinegar. Take care not to stay too close to the patient.

Quoted in Judith Herrin, ed., *A Medieval Miscellany.* New York: Viking Studio, 1999, p. 138.

so much as the first group nor did they fall into such dissoluteness and drunkenness as the second; rather, they satisfied their appetites to a moderate degree. They did not shut themselves up, but went around carrying in their hands flowers, or sweet-smelling herbs, or various kinds of spices; and they would often put these things to their noses, believing that such smells were a wonderful means of purifying the brain, for all the air seemed infected with the stench of dead bodies, sickness, and medicines.

Others were of a crueler opinion (though it was, perhaps, a safer one): they maintained that there was no better medicine against the plague than to flee from it; convinced of this reasoning and caring only about themselves, men and women in great numbers abandoned their city, their houses, their farms, their relatives, and their possessions and sought other places, going at least as far away as the Florentine countryside—as if the wrath of God could not pursue them with this pestilence wherever they went but would only strike those it found within the walls of the city! Or perhaps they thought that Florence's last hour had come and that no one in the city would remain alive.

Avoiding the Sick and Dying

And not all those who adopted these diverse opinions died, nor did they all escape with their lives; on the contrary, many of those who thought this way were falling sick everywhere, and since they had given, when they were healthy, the bad example of avoiding the sick, they in turn were abandoned and left to languish away without any care. The fact was that one citizen avoided another, that almost no one cared for his neighbor, and that relatives rarely or hardly ever visited each other—they stayed far apart. This disaster had struck such fear into the hearts of men and women that brother abandoned brother, uncle abandoned nephew, sister left brother, and very often wife abandoned husband, and—even worse, almost unbelievable—fathers and mothers neglected to tend and care for their children as if they were not their own.

Thus, for the countless multitude of men and women who fell sick, there remained no support except the charity of their friends (and these were few) or the greed of servants, who worked for inflated salaries without regard to the service they performed and who, in spite of this, were few and far between; and those few were men or women of little wit (most of them not trained for such service) who did little else but hand different things to the sick when requested to do so or watch over them while they died, and in this service, they very often lost their own lives and their profits. And since the sick were abandoned by their neighbors, their parents, and their friends and there was a scarcity of servants, a practice that was previously almost unheard of spread through the city: when a woman fell sick, no matter how attractive or beautiful or noble she might be, she did not mind having a manservant (whoever he might be, no matter how young or old he was), and she had no shame whatsoever in revealing any part of her body to him—the way she would have done to a woman—when necessity of her sickness required her to do so. This practice was, perhaps, in the days that followed the pestilence, the cause of looser morals in the women who survived the plague. And so, many people died who, by chance, might have survived if they had been attended to. Between the lack of competent attendants that the sick were unable to obtain and the violence of the pestilence itself, so many, many people died in the city both day and night that it was incredible just to hear this described, not to mention seeing it! Therefore, out of sheer necessity, there arose among those who remained alive customs which were contrary to the established practices of the time. . . .

So Many Corpses . . .

The plight of the lower class and, perhaps, a large part of the middle class was even more pathetic: most of them stayed in their homes or neighborhoods either because of their poverty or because of their hopes for remaining safe, and every day they fell sick by the thousands; and not having servants or attendants of any kind, they almost always died. Many ended their lives in the public streets, during the day or at night, while many others who died in their homes were discovered dead by their neighbors only by the smell of their decomposing bodies. The city was full of corpses. The dead were usually given the same treatment by their neighbors, who were moved more by the fear that the decomposing corpses would contaminate them than by any charity they might have felt toward the deceased: either by themselves or with the assistance of porters (when they were available), they would drag the corpse out of the home and place it in front of the doorstep, where, usually in the morning, quantities of dead bodies could be seen by any passerby; then they were laid out on biers, or for lack of biers, on a plank. Nor did a bier carry only one corpse; sometimes it was used for two or three at a time. More than once, a single bier would serve for a wife and husband, two or three brothers, a father or son, or other relatives, all at the same time. And very often it happened that two priests, each with a cross, would be on their way to bury someone, when porters carrying three or four biers would just follow along behind them; and whereas these priests thought they had just one dead man to bury, they had, in fact, six or eight and sometimes more. Moreover, the dead were honored with no tears or candles or funeral mourners; in fact, things had reached such a point that the people who died were cared for as we care for goats today. Thus it became quite obvious that the very thing which in normal times wise men had not been able to resign themselves to, even though then it struck seldom and less harshly, became as a result of this colossal misfortune a matter of indifference to even the most simpleminded people.

So many corpses would arrive in front of a church every day and at every hour that the amount of holy ground for burials was certainly insufficient for the ancient custom of giving each body its individual place; when all the graves were full, huge trenches were dug in all of the cemeteries of the churches and into them the new arrivals were dumped by the hundreds; and they were packed in there with dirt, one on top of another, like a ship's cargo, until the trench was filled.

Death Arrives in the Countryside

But instead of going over every detail of the past miseries which befell our city, let me say that the hostile winds blowing there did not, however, spare the surrounding countryside any evil; there, not to speak of the towns which, on a smaller scale, were like the city, in the scattered villages and in the fields the poor, miserable peasants and their families, without any medical assistance or aid of servants, died on the roads and in their fields and in their homes, as many by day as by night, and they died not like men but more like animals. Because of this they, like the city dwellers, became careless in their ways and did not look after their possessions or their businesses; furthermore, when they saw that death was upon them, completely neglecting the future fruits of their past labors, their livestock, their property, they did their best to consume what they already had at hand. So it came about that oxen, donkeys, sheep, pigs, chickens, and even dogs, man's most faithful companion, were driven from their homes into the fields, where the wheat was left not only unharvested but also unreaped, and they were allowed to roam where they wished; and many of these animals, almost as if they were rational beings, returned at night to their homes without any guidance from a shepherd, full after a good day's meal.

Leaving the countryside and returning to the city, what more can one say except that so great was the cruelty of Heaven, and, perhaps, also that of man, that from March to July of the same year, between the fury of the pestiferous sickness and the fact that many of the sick were badly treated or abandoned in need because of the fear that the healthy had, more than one hundred thousand human beings are believed to have lost their lives for certain inside the walls of the city of Florence—whereas before the deadly plague, one would not even have estimated there were actually that many people dwelling in the city.

The Ostracized Lepers

Peter Lewis Allen

Leprosy, a disease that disfigures and cripples those afflicted, was widespread in medieval times. The frightful disfigurement inspired terror in the medieval populace. Medieval medicine was limited; therefore, the cause of leprosy was viewed as a punishment from God for the leper's sins. This attitude resulted in the isolation of the leper within his or her own society. Lepers were not allowed to mingle with anyone not similarly afflicted. Lepers could not speak to others and had to wear a clapper to warn others of their approach. Leprosy was one of the most feared diseases during medieval times. Author Peter Lewis Allen, who has written other historical books and is an associate at McKinsey and Company, profiles the leper in his medieval habitat. Allen outlines the rituals in which the church and society engaged in order to condemn the leper to a life of total isolation.

"Death was omnipresent" [in the Middle Ages], writes historian D.H. Pennington, "and witnessing it was everyone's experience." Beyond the ever-present reality of malnutrition, people suffered from many diseases, including plague, fevers, scrofula, and tuberculosis. All of these were brutal, but one of the diseases they feared most was the slow and loathsome disintegration of leprosy.

Leprosy was an African disease that had become endemic in Europe by the end of the sixth century. It terrified people because it was disfiguring, disgusting, and mysterious in whom it chose to afflict. Some physicians believed the disease was hereditary; others said it was spread by contagion, although scientific and medical theory could not really explain how contagion worked. Some believed that sexual intercourse transmitted or caused the hideous affliction. No matter what they thought was its source, many people believed that leprosy came straight from God to punish humanity for its sins.

Peter Lewis Allen, *The Wages of Sin: Sex and Disease, Past and Present.* Chicago, IL: University of Chicago Press, 2000.

This belief was so strong, and the patterns it etched so searing, that they remained deep in the European heart for centuries. A century and more after leprosy had departed from Western Europe, moldering medieval leper hospitals were reopened to serve as isolation wards for the corrupt souls and bodies of heretics and syphilitics. Decrepit, isolated, and accursed, the medieval leper remained for centuries a symbol of the worst that God could visit on humanity.

Punishment for Sinning

Spreading slowly throughout the body, the leprosy bacterium damages the nerves and keeps the blood from supplying oxygen and nutrients to the skin; secondary infections descend on dying flesh like birds of prey on carrion. First they raise unsightly calluses and scars; then fingers, toes, and sections of nasal tissue fall away. Hands and feet are twisted into bear-claw shapes; the face becomes broken and twisted; nasal cartilage and vocal cords are damaged, and the voice becomes raspy and honking. As tubercular lesions protrude, the eyebrows become swollen and denuded of hair; the face, the skin, and the limbs take on frightening new aspects; the mouth and nostrils become twisted; the eyes take on a horrifying stare; and breath and body often give off a disgusting smell.

With these stark and offensive transformations, it is hardly surprising that the impulse to fear, loathe, and isolate lepers was ancient and enduring. . . .

This pattern was not universal: lepers were allowed to roam freely in Byzantium and in the medieval Islamic world. But ancient Greek historians noted that other cultures they observed would not tolerate lepers among the general population. Pausanias, in 479 B.C., recorded that a town in Elida was called Leproon because so many lepers lived there; in Persia, Herodotus (484?–425? B.C.) observed, lepers were driven from cities. The ten lepers Jesus healed in Luke 17 "stood afar off" from him while begging to be healed; the Greek doctors of the sixth and seventh centuries A.D. noted that their cities drove lepers away. Some of this separation was no doubt caused simply by revulsion, and some of it may have been caused by medical fears, but in Europe, at least, the greatest concern was sin. As medical historian Katharine Park explains, medieval European laws "aimed to set lepers apart as foci of moral and ritual defilement rather than as threats to public health." The ruin leprosy inflicted on people's bodies reflected in some way God's judgment on their souls, and most people wanted to have little to do with either.

Isolating the Leper

The twelfth and thirteenth centuries were the height of the disease's spread in Europe, and the laws of these years often reflected people's desire to put the safety of distance between themselves and the afflicted—especially those who were both afflicted and poor. The laws of the kingdom of Navarre in 1155 ordered those lepers who could not support themselves to "beg alms in the city, outside doors, using the noise of the clappers" alone to solicit the attention and charity of passers-by, avoiding all conversation with children and the young. The Third Lateran Council (1179) relegated lepers to "solitary places" outside the walls of cities and towns. By 1220, notes one historian, "it was a civil crime for a leper to dwell among the healthy," and in 1278 the laws of Metz set up an elaborate intelligence system for weeding out lepers, with serious penalties for those who failed to cooperate. A leper who did not turn himself in would have an ear cut off; the citizen who gave him alms was fined. Police who failed to turn lepers in were subject to severe strictures; a citizen of Calais is recorded as having been punished for sheltering his leprous brother.

Cities and countries passed laws that drove the afflicted out. The twelfth-century Burrow laws and thirteenth-century Church canons expelled lepers from Scotland. Gloucester expelled lepers in 1273, London in 1276, Bristol in 1344, and Norwich in 1375; the Scots parliament in 1427 forbade lepers to beg in town. Paris banned them in 1321, 1371, 1388, 1394, 1402, and 1403—so often, in fact, that one prominent French historian suggests that the bans cannot have been very effective. Effective or no, however, this insistent legislation testified to the fact that, even if lepers remained in town, they were as unwelcome as rats.

Those laws that did not send lepers out of town made certain that they were easy to spot and avoid. In some areas, lepers (like Jews) were made to wear yellow badges; in others, the markers were red. To avoid soiling even the dirt in the medieval streets—streets that often flowed with raw sewage and the blood of animals slaughtered in butchers' stalls—lepers were forced to wear shoes at all times. They had to carry a clapper or a bell to warn people to keep their distance. They could not touch items in the market; instead, they had to point them out with a long pole. Begging was a necessity for them, but it was also exceptionally difficult. Lepers had to use their poles to retrieve their begging cups from the side of the road, since they were not allowed to approach those whom they solicited for farthings and crusts of bread. The citizens of Arras, in France, made official complaints when they caught lepers handling the fruit in vendors' baskets in the town market. Without being quite willing to let the diseased starve in the woods, Europeans did everything they could not to have to touch, speak with, interact with, or even see those marked by this malady of body and soul.

A Bit of Kindness

Those who were more compassionate tried to find a middle way, setting up a broad array of charitable hospitals to shelter the sick. The number of these leper houses reached a high-water mark in medieval Europe, but the tradition had started far earlier. Leper hospitals, in fact, were among the earliest medical establishments in the West.

Hospitals were born from the central Christian values of charity and healing. By the third century A.D., urban Christians had organized large-scale efforts to help the poor and the sick, and in the fourth century the first Western hospital had been founded by St. Basil of Caesarea, who had studied medicine in Athens. Basil welcomed strangers, the crippled, and lepers to his care, and would greet his patients with a kiss before treating their afflictions and dressing their wounds himself. In the fourth century, a wealthy Roman noble established a hospital specifically for lepers, and the emperor Constantius soon built another. This prototype gave rise to two different models. In Byzantium—and, following this model, in Islam—Basil's charity toward the sick combined with the traditions of Greek medicine, and produced hospitals primarily focused on medical care. Islamic hospitals also devoted resources to pharmacy, clinical training, mental health, and research, and, being essentially secular institutions, they were able to enhance their staffs by hiring Christian and Jewish physicians.

Hospitals in Western Europe followed quite a different path. They viewed themselves essentially as religious institutions dedicated to providing charity in accordance with Christian views; medical care was only incidental to this mission. Some hospitals, for example, lodged and fed poor travelers (though only for a night or two; after that, the vagrants were sent on their way). Others took on the responsibility of keeping poor women out of the clutches of vice. Statutes were written to ensure that hospital inmates behaved properly: charity was dispensed to the poor only when they adhered to the strict laws of virtue.

Gradually, hospitals became more specialized. Some focused on providing temporary shelter for the poor, while some housed and cared for the sick; in France, the latter were called Hôtels-Dieu, Houses of God. Others were specifically built to house, on a more permanent basis, those who suffered from the incurable affliction of leprosy. The earliest English leper houses were founded before 1100; in Scotland and France, the first establishments began in the twelfth century, probably in response to the increasing preva-

This woodcut depicts a sixteenth-century hospital in Paris. Known as Hôtels-Dieu, they provided care in accordance with Christian views.

lence of the disease. Their numbers grew rapidly: by the death of the French king Louis VIII in 1226, there were 1,000 leper houses in France, and Louis IX (St. Louis, 1214–1270) founded 340 more. These mostly small establishments were deliberately kept humble, and their furnishings could not fail to remind the "brothers" and "sisters" of why they were there. The regulations of the late twelfth-century English leper house of Sherburne, for example, ordered that "in the house itself, they should have four lead cisterns, four pans, four tripods, two tubs, one broom, and a spade for burying the dead." Some French leper houses were painted red to warn off unwary passers-by. . . .

Expulsion

Nobody expected lepers to recover from their condition: the leprosaria simply sheltered them until they died. As Katharine Park has crisply observed, these institutions "were charitable rather than therapeutic." And charity was strictly defined: as in other hospitals, strict obedience was required in all matters. The statutes of the leper house of Amiens, dating from 1305, ordained that "if any of the brothers or sisters does anything dishonorable, he will be punished at the master's will according to the counsel of the brothers."

The lepers had considerable authority in this area, in fact. Some people came to leper houses of their own accord; others were turned in when people denounced them to the public authorities. Sometimes, parents even brought in their own children. However they came, those suspected of leprosy had to be judged by a panel of experts made up of the lepers themselves; only in the fifteenth century did doctors and surgeons join the tribunal. The judgment was taken very seriously. The men and women who served on the panel had to swear to judge accurately; if they refused to participate, they could be fined. The examinations were as scientific as the knowledge of the day permitted. There was a comprehensive visual inspection (leper houses even had a special heated room so that in winter suspects could be examined without their clothes), followed by blood and urine tests; sometimes suspects were sent to other leper houses for a second opinion. Both lepers and physicians were reluctant to misdiagnose, since, for most lepers, the sentence was irreversible.

Not all lepers were able to reside in leper houses, which were usually reserved for citizens of the cities that had built them. All others—unless their families made a substantial gift to the endowment—were condemned to wander the world and beg for their sustenance. As a result, the severest punishment the administrators could impose was expulsion—cutting lepers off from food, shelter, and the only human society they were allowed to join.

Of the many things lepers could do wrong, two provoked the greatest anxiety: running away and having sex. Often, these misadventures were viewed as related: statutes forbade spending the night anywhere but under the administrators' watchful eye. For passing a night in town, Amiens would expel lepers for a year and a day, and then impose forty days' penance on them when they returned. Leper houses in the British Isles were even more severe, as historian Charles Arthur Mercier records: "At Greenside, in Scotland, the same offense was a hanging matter, and lest any leper should plead that he knew not, or had forgotten the penalty, the authorities thoughtfully set up a gibbet before the gate of the hospital to remind him."

The Sin of Lust

These punishments were stringent for a reason: leprosy had been associated with sin since biblical times. King Ozias, in 2 Chronicles, had been punished with leprosy for his sacrilege; the early Church had viewed the disease as a punishment for violations of sacred law. St. Ambrose said that the Jews had been eaten away by leprosy of the body and the soul, and the will of St. Ephrem (d. 373) threatened with leprosy anyone who disturbed his remains or doubted the Church. Other Church fathers also saw leprosy as the wages of sin: Jerome claimed it was God's punishment for the original transgression of Adam and Eve, while St. Caesarius of Arles (ca. 470–542) invoked it upon the children of men who violated the chastity the Church required of them during Lent, major festivals, or the pregnancy and menstrual periods of their wives. Gregory of Tours (538–593) told a story about a thief who stole from a church and was stricken with leprosy as a result. Documents from the eleventh and twelfth centuries described leprosy as God's recompense for blasphemous and cruel acts, and Odo of Cheriton (ca. 1180–1247) retold the story of the original sin with a leper in the place of the serpent.

Most of all, leprosy was tied to the sin of lust. This belief, too, had early Christian roots. Lactantius (ca. 250–325, defender of Christianity against Roman attacks) said that those who sinned because of their insatiable desires should be treated as lepers. Rightly or wrongly—physicians still disagree—leprosy was embroiled in a confusion with sexually transmitted diseases, a belief that can be traced back to fifth-century India and was commonplace in twelfth-century European medical writings. Christian authors of the same era, including the profoundly influential St. Bernard of Clairvaux, believed that leprosy afflicted the children of promiscuous parents. By the sixteenth century, some physicians called the disease "satyriasis," believing that it was linked with this state of continuous and painful sexual arousal. The Italian physician Girolamo Fracastoro (1478–1553) even claimed that, because eunuchs rarely suffered from leprosy, some people castrated themselves in a desperate quest for immunity from the dread disease. Medieval laws imposed harsh penalties on lepers who had sex with prostitutes, and a leprosy diagnosis rendered marriages null and void. Some twelfth-century Christian writers, such as Hildegard of Bingen and William of Conches (d. after 1145) even associated leprosy with melancholy, the root cause of lovesickness, saying that the skin disease was caused by an excess of black bile in the blood.

These beliefs ensured that chastity was strictly enforced on lepers. The leper house of Meaux, for example, founded in the late twelfth century, required that a male resident found with a woman at night do humiliating penance by eating bread and water on the ground, "at the master's pleasure." Those who went past simple fraternization and were actually caught *in flagrante delicto* were imprisoned or expelled. In the leper house at Andelys, men who fornicated were expelled for a year and a day from the food and shelter the hospice provided; women who became pregnant were expelled or imprisoned "forever." The house at Lille prohibited not only marriage, but also lust and simple infatuation. Even lepers who had been married were forbidden to have sex—even if their spouses were devoted enough to take up residence in the hospice. Married couples lived and slept apart;

their only common activity was the sharing of lunch once a week; all sexual contact was forbidden. . . .

The Living Dead

The fear and superstition lepers aroused gave them a strange status: they were not members of society, but neither were they altogether out of mind. Both civil and religious law wrestled with this uneasiness and tried to come up with ways of placing these troubled souls into a condition that reflected society's views. Morally, socially, legally, and religiously, lepers were the living dead, whom God had marked out and who could no longer be part of human society, yet who still walked the earth. . . .

Regardless of whether people—both laymen and ecclesiastics—believed lepers were blessed or cursed, the one thing they were sure of was that they did not want lepers in their towns. Laws expelling them from cities were one attempt to keep their festering sores out of view; building leper houses was another, more charitable, approach. But starker and more chilling were the ceremonies of separation the Church developed in the later Middle Ages to teach lepers to stay out of the lives of ordinary folk and to remind the latter that lepers were truly members of the dead.

First, the leper was wrapped in a shroud; then he or she was carried to a church that had been draped in funereal black, where the priest took a final confession and intoned the solemn liturgy of a requiem mass. The service then moved to the churchyard. Standing in an open grave, the leper was directly addressed by the priest—not in Latin, as usual, but in the vernacular, to avoid any possibility of misunderstanding. Leprosy, explained the priest, was a sign of God's mercy. Rather than waiting until death, the leper was being punished for his or her sins before even departing from this life. Sometimes the priest would scatter a shovelful of earth over the leper's head. The priest then provided the few possessions the invalid would henceforth own. These filled only a short list: a purse, a drinking cup, a food bag, gloves, a cloak, and a wooden clapper, the leper's symbolic new voice, designed to prevent the leper's infecting the air by his or her noisome speech. "See here the tongue the Church has granted you," the priest would explain, "forbidding you to ask for alms except by means of this instrument. And also, the Church forbids you ever to speak to anyone unless you are bidden to speak." . . .

After a few final words of spiritual comfort, the leper was escorted to a special hospice, never to return. His or her will took effect; all property passed to the leper's heirs. Legally widowed, the leper's spouse was free to remarry. The leper was now dead to the world. . . .

The thirteenth and fourteenth centuries were cruel times for many—even those without leprosy. People were hanged for stealing; outlaws could be beaten or killed as freely as dogs; courts sentenced criminals to be dragged to death, beheaded, and even buried alive. At times the blind were treated as a spectacle, paraded through the streets or forced into combat with one another. It was not good to depend on the tender mercies of the public in the late Middle Ages.

Still, no matter how others suffered, it seems likely that lepers suffered more. Their bodies decayed, their faces twisted, their hoarse and honking voices silenced, they wandered from place to place, wanted nowhere and often tolerated less than the garbage and excrement at the side of the road. Cut off from their families (unless these had enough money to keep them in isolation at home), they lost not only their earthly property, their livelihood, their spouses, but also their access to communities of the spirit.

The Jewish Persecution

Heinrich Truchess von Diessenhoven

The medieval medical community was not able to comprehend the causes of the bubonic plague or the reasons for the high mortality rate. Medieval citizens were seized with fear. In their fear, they put the blame on a common target of persecution: Jews. Rumors began spreading in many parts of Europe that Jews were poisoning Christian wells and water supplies, thereby spreading the disease. Amid all the frenzy, no one seemed to notice that the Jews were equally dying of the plague.

In the following selection Heinrich Truchess von Diessenhoven describes the systematic burning of Jews throughout Europe. The author, who was a canon of Constance and had been a chaplain of Pope John XXII during the 1300s, fully endorses the horrific events he recounts.

The persecution of the Jews began in November 1348, and the first outbreak in Germany was at Sölden, where all the Jews were burnt on the strength of a rumour that they had poisoned wells and rivers, as was afterwards confirmed by their own confessions and also by the confessions of Christians whom they had corrupted and who had been induced by the Jews to carry out the deed. And some of the Jews who were newly baptised said the same. Some of these remained in the faith but some others relapsed, and when these were placed upon the wheel [a method of torture] they confessed that they had themselves sprinkled poison or poisoned rivers. And thus no doubt remained of their deceitfulness which had now been revealed.

The Burning of the Jews

Within the revolution of one year, that is from All Saints [1 November] 1348 until Michaelmas [29 September] 1349 all the

---

Heinrich Truchess von Diessenhoven, *The Black Death*, translated and edited by Rosemary Horrox. New York: Manchester University Press, 1994.

Jews between Cologne and Austria were burnt and killed for this crime, young men and maidens and the old along with the rest. And blessed be God who confounded the ungodly who were plotting the extinction of his church, not realising that it is founded on a sure rock and who, in trying to overturn it, crushed themselves to death and were damned for ever.

But now let us follow the killings individually. First Jews were killed or burnt in Sölden in November, then in Zofingen they were seized and some put on the wheel, then in Stuttgart they were all burnt. The same thing happened during November in Landsberg, a town in the diocese of Augsburg and in Bueron, Memmingen and Burgau [all cities named are in Germany] in the same diocese. During December they were burnt and killed on the feast of St Nicholas [6 December] in Lindau, on 8 December in Reutlingen, on 13 December in Haigerloch, and on 20 December in Horw they were burnt in a pit. And when the wood and straw had been consumed, some Jews, both young and old, still remained half alive. The stronger of them snatched up cudgels and stones and dashed out the brains of those trying to creep out of the fire, and thus compelled those who wanted to escape the fire to descend to hell. And the curse seemed to be fulfilled: 'his blood be upon us and upon our children' [a biblical reference].

On 27 December the Jews in Esslingen were burnt in their houses and in the synagogue. In *Nagelten* they were burnt. In the abovesaid town of Zofingen the city councillors, who were hunting for poison, found some in the house of a Jew called Trostli, and by experiment were satisfied that it was poison. As a result, two Jewish men and one woman were put on the wheel, but others were saved at the command of Duke Albrecht of Austria, who ordered that they should be protected. But this made little difference, for in the course of the next year those he had under his protection were killed, and as many again in the diocese of Constance. But first those burnt in 1349 will be described in order.

The Fury Continues

Once started, the burning of the Jews went on increasing. When people discovered that the stories of poisoning were undoubtedly true they rose as one against the Jews. First, on 2 January 1349 the citizens of Ravensburg burnt the Jews in the castle, to which they had fled in search of protection from King Charles, whose servants were imprisoned by the citizens after the burning. On 4 January the people of Constance shut up the Jews in two of their own houses, and then burnt 330 of them in the fields at sunset on 3 March. Some processed to the flames dancing, others singing and the rest weeping. They were burnt shut up in a house which had been specially built for the purpose. On 12 January in Buchen and on 17 January in Basel they were all burnt apart from their babies, who were taken from them by the citizens and baptised. They were burnt on 21 January in Messkirch and Waldkirch, on 25 January in Speyer, and on 30 January in Ulm, on 11 February in Überlingen, on 14 February in the city of Strassburg (where it took six days to burn them because of the numbers involved), on 16 February in Mengen, on 19th of the month in Sulgen, on 21st in Schaffhausen and Zurich, on 23rd in St Gallen and on 3 March in Constance, as described above, except for some who were kept back to be burnt on the third day after the Nativity of the Virgin [11 September].

They were killed and burnt in the town of Baden on 18 March, and those in the castle below, who had been brought there from Rheinfelden for protection, were killed and then burnt. And on 30 May they were similarly wiped out in Radolfzell. In Mainz and Cologne they were burnt on 23 August. On 18 September 330 Jews were burnt in the castle at Kyburg, where they had gathered from Winterthur and Diessenhoven and the other towns of their protector the Duke of Austria. But the imperial citizens did not want to go on supporting them any longer, and so they wrote to Duke Albrecht of Austria, who was protecting his Jewish subjects in the counties of Pfirt, Alsace and Kyburg, and told him that either he had them burnt by his own judges or they would burn them themselves. So the Duke ordered them to be burnt by his own judges, and they were finally burnt on 18 September.

And thus, within one year, as I said, all the Jews between Cologne and Austria were burnt—and in Austria they await the same fate, for they are accursed of God. And I could believe that the end of the Hebrews had come, if the time prophesied by Elias and Enoch were now complete; but since it is not complete, it is necessary that some be reserved so that what has been written may be fulfilled: that the hearts of the sons shall be turned to their fathers, and of the fathers to the sons. But in what parts of the world they may be reserved I do not know, although I think it more likely that the seed of Abraham will be reserved in lands across the sea than in these people. So let me make an end of the Jews here.

Crimes and Hazards During the Middle Ages

Carolly Erickson

The Middle Ages was a time of great social disorder. Medieval citizens had to cope with wars, criminal bands, famine, fires, floods, and corrupt officials. The lack of a police force or an effective communication system allowed criminals free reign to kill, maim, rape, and plunder. Not only was the medieval populace at the mercy of criminal bands, but it was also subject to natural disasters such as fire. Since towns were built mostly of wood, fire was a constant threat to home and life. It was not uncommon for fires to destroy the same town many times during a decade. In the following excerpt author Carolly Erickson, who has written other books, including *The Records of Medieval Europe*, discusses the various crimes that plagued medieval citizens and the lack of control the government had over punishing these crimes.

In the middle decades of the fourteenth century, parts of England were overrun with criminal bands whose members were drawn from both gentry and ordinary folk and whose powerful supporters employed them, fed them, and hid them from the judges and agents sent out by the court of king's bench. Like their employment, their numbers varied, but on major campaigns they grew to the size of armies. Testifying to events he had watched, the bishop of Exeter told how a great force of men arrayed like soldiers marched on his lands, breaking fences and gates before them and seizing hundreds of bullocks, cows and sheep and other things of value. The villagers fled in panic, thinking the plunderers were a foreign army of invaders foraging for food.

No road or public place was secure from the assaults of those who "rode armed publicly and secretly in manner of war by day

Carolly Erickson, *The Medieval Vision: Essays in History and Perception*. New York: Oxford University Press, 1976.

and night." Roads were ordered cleared of hedges for 200 feet on either side, and roadside ditches filled in, to prevent ambushes. Nevertheless, merchants and others were set upon in their shops as well as on the roads, and brigands on horseback rode straight through fair grounds at the height of fairs, overturning booths and stealing their contents and leaving behind them a burning town. Sometimes the assaults took the form of a private war between royal officials and the outlaws, with ordinary citizens only incidental victims of their struggle. Thus William Beckwith and his outlawed relatives and followers, some five hundred strong, held out against the king's justices in Lancaster for five years at the end of the fourteenth century, but for at least the last two they kept to the deep woods and did not molest men on the road or in their homes.

Beckwith's men were unusual in that they were almost exclusively servants, tradesmen and poor tenants who turned to outlawry. Most English criminal bands contained a sizable proportion of knights or knights' sons, and nearly every outlaw company had the support of powerful titled men.

The best documented of these bands grew around the six wayward sons of John de Folville, lord of Ashby-Folville in Leicestershire. (The seventh, who succeeded to his father's lands and eventually entered the local justice system as a keeper of the peace, had no part in their activities.) One of the six brothers, Richard Folville, was rector of a parish church; the others took solely to crime. The most infamous of the Folvilles, Eustace, was undoubtedly responsible for five murders (probably more) and a long list of thefts, assaults, rapes and extortion schemes. With several or all of his five outlawed brothers, Eustace murdered a baron of the Exchequer and a number of lesser men, kidnapped a royal judge, and was implicated in dozens of robberies and property damage suits over a period of nearly twenty years. . . .

Among the early employers of the Folvilles were a canon of Sempringham and the cellarer of the Cistercian house of Haverholm, who hired the outlaws for £20 to destroy a water mill and later sheltered them from discovery. Other employers included Sir William Aune, a Yorkshire constable, Sir Robert Ingram, mayor of Nottingham and sheriff of Nottinghamshire, the chapter of Lichfield Cathedral, and at least four royal bailiffs and seven members of parliament. In all, hundreds of people were cited as sometime abettors of the Folvilles and their collateral followers, but despite several determined forays by royal justices and their agents, most of the criminals avoided capture. Richard Folville was finally murdered outside his church by a local keeper of the peace, but the most notorious brother, Eustace, died a natural death in 1346, by which time he had become a prominent landed knight. The other brothers make their last appearance in the records as mercenaries in the pay of the king, bound for Flanders.

Fearlessness Among the Criminals

The ease with which outlaws were able to obtain pardons or ransom their crimes by joining the royal army helps to explain their fearlessness. Outlawed in 1326 for the murder of a baron of the Exchequer, the Folvilles were pardoned at the beginning of Edward III's reign in 1327 to show the new king's magnanimity. A few years later, after the gang was outlawed again for murder, robbery and rape they were able to earn another pardon, issued generally to all who had helped to put down the rebellion of the earl of Lancaster. Following their boldest crime, the kidnap and ransom of the royal justice Richard Wylughby in 1332, Robert Folville was pardoned in exchange for "good services in the Scottish war." And it was as pardoned felons that Richard, Walter and Thomas Folville, with James and Nicholas Coterel, went with the king to Flanders in 1338.

Though they were not narrowly political in origin the crimes of the Folvilles and Coterels were certainly urged on by the political unrest in the early years of Edward III's reign. There is some evidence that the former enjoyed some favor with the courtiers of Mortimer, lover of the dowager queen and co-regent, and the latter were hired to devastate the manors of Henry of Lancaster, leader of the baronial opposition to Mortimer in the late 1320's. But they did not become outlaws as a direct result of the uncertain political situation. Rather they found that as enforcement of order grew more and more lax, and popular contempt for royal officials more and more pronounced, a rift opened in the social fabric, creating an extra-legal enclave within which criminality was both feared for its reinlessness and applauded for its open defiance of the agents of public order. In their haughtiest crime the Folvilles and Coterels waylaid Richard Wylughby, puisne justice of the court of King's Bench, while he was on a judicial commission in the southwest and held him until a ransom of 1300 marks was paid. Only one of the accessories to the crime was brought to justice, and the outlaws grew in public favor for punishing a hated judge who "sold the law like cows and oxen."

Dysfunctional Governments

In their recurring crises the fragile governments of the middle ages were quick to lose the power of legal retribution they built up in times of stability. In these periods the pursuit of criminals and their trying and sentencing were all but suspended; the present impact of the king's justice lapsed, and those who lived outside the law grew in numbers and ambition.

In later fourteenth and fifteenth-century England the enclaves of impunity created by governmental crises eventually threatened to absorb the entire kingdom, and took on institutional form. Through the practices of maintenance (illegal coercion applied by a powerful man to influence the trial of a lesser associate), embracery (physical violence to prevent a jury from bringing an indictment) and the wearing of livery (uniforms of the private armies of magnates), a new system of personal protection, retribution and armed defense was superimposed on the existing social bonds. Those who sought to destroy it suddenly found that the very basis of power had shifted its ground, leaving them powerless. The royal court, the law courts and the parliament were riddled with magnates and their liveried retainers. Highly placed officials under the protection of the magnates could intercept petitions for reform, and bands of armed retainers could break open any court, council or parliamentary session and scatter the participants. Strangled in this new web of alliances, the traditional workings of government withered, while liveried retainers, mercenaries without a war, became the sole levers of power.

But few eras witnessed social disruption this acute. Maintenance represented crime on its grandest scale, with the high ambition to challenge the very foundations of public order. Less grandiose crimes—theft, rape, murder, committed against individuals by individuals—were commoner, and showed less fluctuation from decade to decade. Crimes of this sort were an expected hazard of life, part of the unexceptional nameless violence that formed an important dimension of the medieval world view.

A Violent Life

For along with their finely developed sense of order and of the ideal social hierarchy medieval people tolerated a degree of anarchy, violence and loss of life that is difficult for us to comprehend. Transcribing the plea rolls for 1221, the great legal historian Frederick Maitland found that in four Gloucester hundreds, forty murders were recorded, plus one suicide and three accidental deaths. Fully half the murders were committed by unknown persons who fled before their crimes were discovered; of those who were known, only one was captured, brought to trial, and hanged. (One other claimed the right of sanctuary and abjured the realm.) Murder was by far the commonest crime; in all, for 1221 the rolls list only eighteen thefts, three accusations of rape and fifteen cases of fraud, assault, and petty infractions.

What is striking in these judicial records is the variety and frequency of violent death: knife-murders, axe-murders, murders by bludgeoning with a stone; murder of a fetus through an assault on a pregnant woman (occasioning a legal debate over whether or not a woman may bring an appeal for the death of her unborn child); murders of close kin (murder of brother by brother, wife by husband, son by mother); murder of a man by his horse (whose value in coin was offered to the church as compensation). Two men are found slain by unknown assailants, the chaplain is drowned returning from a banquet, the reeve's servant dies from a fall, a serf falls from a horse and is killed—again the horse's value must be paid as compensation. A woman is brought into court and accused of concealing the unburied corpse of her husband who died of plague, but she herself dies soon afterward and the case is not pursued. Two pilgrims take shelter in the hundred of Holeford; overnight one kills the other and flees, and neither the victim nor his attacker can be identified.

There was nothing unique about the level of crime in thirteenth-century Gloucester. Plea roll entries for a single Norfolk hundred, North Erpingham, over a twelve-month period two generations later list some fifty major crimes, with twelve men and women murdered by unknowns, five dying in fatal fights, and five more by suicide. Sixteen burglars were tried; one man was torn to pieces by horses for debasing the coin, the eleven others were hanged for various grave offenses. There are gang murders in these rolls too, and records of criminal families. In one of these families the leading offender is jailed in a wooden house; his young son tries to free him by setting fire to the house, but is trapped in the flames. The father escapes, only to be caught and executed. . . .

Piracy, armed coercion, blatant and subtle violence were strong and constant forces in medieval life. The fourteenth-century Irish archbishop Richard Fitzralph, calculating his clergy's share in the spiritual commerce of the church, noted that in his diocese alone some two thousand "evildoers" came to his attention each year, many of whom sought and obtained (on slight repentance) pardon for their sins before God. And a recent student of medieval criminality in England, John Bellamy, concluded that "not one investigator has been able to indicate even a few years of effective policing" between 1285 and the end of the fifteenth century.

An Earthly Life of Misfortune and Loss

The inescapable evidence of disrule was reflected very faithfully in medieval historiography. Chronicles written thousands of miles apart evoke the same catastrophic view of history, a view which merged the ravages of criminality, with the broader destruction of floods, droughts, famine, murrain and plague. Their accounts of human affairs, which often seem to leap from crime to hazard to disaster, were fully in harmony with their providential bias: crises and sudden death were necessary forms of divine retribution for sin, reminders of the transience of all earthly life. But none of these events were included solely to edify; they were seen as noteworthy elements in the human record, awesome burdens inseparable from the course of secular affairs.

So often the events which medieval writers put in the foreground of their histories are those modern historians look past in their reading of these records. Yet to look past them is to overlook not only the real or exaggerated details of long-past tragedies but also the climate of insecurity they produced. Medieval people lived in expectation of misfortune and loss—an expectation made more pronounced by an accompanying conviction of helplessness. Within this frame of expectation, the present seemed vulnerable to innumerable hazards and the future uncertain at best, and even good fortune seemed fleeting and precarious.

The temper I mean to describe here is not one of unrelieved despair; rather it is an attitude to experience which greatly respects the power of unaccountable disaster, and is never free of its menace. It is neither optimism nor pessimism, but an ingrained awe in the familiar presence of bad fortune. At the heart of this attitude was a deep awareness that disease, suffering and calamity were inexorable; once they struck, they would take their own course, unrestrained by men.

And in fact it is difficult to imagine the destructive power these forces had in the past. The threat and wreck of fire in medieval towns are particularly hard to conceive. Whether caused by lightning, accidents with cooking fires, candles or arsonists, fires begun in the densely built wooden structures of medieval towns spread rapidly from one street to the next and one quarter to the next. "The only plagues of London," wrote William Fitz Stephen in his description of the city in the late twelfth century, "are the immoderate drinking of fools and the frequency of fires."

The reaction of the populace was not to try to put such fires out but to salvage their possessions and flee, and indeed, the odds against the former were so great that flight was the only sensible reaction. Stone buildings were always sought out as safe refuges, yet even these usually had some wood in their construction, and did not offer any protection against smoke and heat. City chronicles record the frequency and extent of urban fires; over the three centuries covered by the Novgorod chronicle, the city was largely destroyed by fire several times (omitting fires started by invaders) with ten more devastating blazes obliterating extensive areas and twelve leveling one or more entire neighborhoods. Twenty-two lesser fires, destroying several streets, the entire marketplace or the commercial areas where the Scandinavians and other westerners lived and traded, were also recorded. But in their catalogues of destruction the chroniclers set down not only the streets and churches and suburbs affected, but the panic of the victims as well. During the great firestorm of 1340 that burned most of the city, the monastic scribe (who was not given to gratuitous rhetoric) wrote that

> so great and fierce was the fire, with storm and gale, that the people thought it was the end of the world; the fire went burning over the water, and many people were drowned in the Volga; and the fire threw itself across the Volga to the other side and there by evening service time the whole of that side rapidly burned, from the Fedor stream into Slavno and up to the fields, . . . and whatever anyone brought out and laid either in the fields or in the gardens, or in the fosse or in boats or canoes, all was taken by the flames; and whatever else was brought out wicked men carried it off, who fear not God, nor expect the resurrection of the dead. . . .

Though they shared with other medieval populations a pervasive undercurrent of apprehension, the citizens of Novgorod were not pessimists or cynics. Churchmen and nobles and merchants of the city continued to build several new wooden (and fewer stone) churches every year, and to rebuild the damaged neighborhoods around them, even though they must have known that much of what they built risked almost certain destruction within a generation. Pessimism and cynicism go beyond the hovering anticipation of disaster to deny the significance of good fortune as well. The medievals were not suspicious of good fortune, nor were they blind to it, they merely expected little of it, and were reconciled to the constant threat of cureless tragedy along with it.

Chronology

A.D.

337
Roman emperor Constantine the Great dies. The Roman Empire adopts Christianity.

402
Ravenna, Italy, is established as the capital of the western empire.

410
The Sack of Rome by Visigoths is led by Alaric.

418
Visigoths settle in Aquitaine, establishing a capital at Toulouse, France.

476
Romulus Augustulus, the last Roman emperor, is assassinated.

481
Upon the death of King Childeric of the Franks, Clovis ascends to the throne.

496
Clovis, the king of the Franks, converts to Christianity.

507
The Franks conquer the Visigoth kingdom in southwest Gaul (present-day France).

525
The Monte Cassino monastery is founded by Saint Benedict.

527
Slav tribes gradually penetrate the Balkans.

570

Muhammad, the founder of Islam, is born in Arabia.

637

Arabs defeat the Persian Empire.

638

Jerusalem falls to Arabs.

691

Clovis III becomes king of the Franks.

711

The Islamic conquest of Spain begins.

732

Frankish leader Charles Martel defeats the Muslim expansion in France.

742

Charlemagne is born.

800

Charlemagne is crowned emperor.

814

Charlemagne dies and is succeeded by his son, Louis the Pious.

843

The Carolingian Empire is divided among the three sons of Louis the Pious.

870

The Vikings discover Iceland.

948

Otto I of Germany founds missionary bishoprics in German territories.

962
Otto I is crowned Holy Roman Emperor by Pope John XII.

987
Louis V, the last Carolingian king of France, dies.

1000
King Olaf introduces Christianity to Sweden.

1013
The Danes take control of England.

1050
The Normans of France begin raids into England.

1066
Duke William of Normandy defeats and kills King Harold of England at Hastings and gains the English crown.

1095
Pope Urban II proclaims the start of the First Crusade.

1097
The First Crusade reaches Constantinople.

1099
Jerusalem falls to crusaders.

1145
Pope Eugene III proclaims the Second Crusade.

1162
Thomas Becket is elected archbishop of Canterbury.

1163
Work begins on the construction of the gothic cathedral Notre Dame in Paris.

1170

Thomas Becket is assassinated at Canterbury Cathedral by knights sent by King Henry II of England.

1187

The Muslim king Saladin captures Jerusalem and expels the Christians.

1189

The Third Crusade is announced.

1204

Crusaders capture and loot the city of Constantinople.

1215

King John of England agrees to sign the Magna Carta, the document guaranteeing certain political rights, such as no taxation without representation, trial by jury, and protection of the law.

1217–1221

The Fifth Crusade captures and then loses Damietta in Egypt.

1222

The University of Padua is founded in Italy.

1248–1250

Louis IX of France leads a crusade and is captured in Egypt.

1250

Gold coinage is minted in Florence, Italy.

1270

King Louis IX dies while leading the Eighth Crusade.

1271

Marco Polo begins his journey to China.

1306

King Philip IV expels the Jews from France.

1315–1317

Europe experiences harvest failures and famine.

1321

Dante Alighieri, the Florentine poet, dies in Ravenna.

1337

On French soil, the Hundred Years' War begins between England and France.

1347

The bubonic plague breaks out in southern Italy and quickly spreads to Europe, killing one-third of the population of Europe.

1348

Giovanni Boccaccio, Italian author and humanist, writes the *Decameron.*

1355

Stephen Dušan, the ruler of Serbia and a defender of Europe against the Turks, dies.

1358

A peasant uprising known as the *Jacquerie* (after the common peasant name *Jacque*) takes place in France.

1361

The second wave of the bubonic plague begins.

1362

William Langland, the English poet, writes *The Vision of Piers Plowman.*

1365

The University of Vienna is founded by Rudolph, duke of Austria.

1381

The Peasants' Revolt, led by Wat Tyler, begins and ends in England. The rebellion comes to an end with the execution of Tyler.

1431

Joan of Arc of France is burned at the stake by the English.

1453

Constantinople falls to the Turks and is renamed Istanbul; the Hundred Years' War ends with France driving the English out of France entirely (except for the port city of Calais); Johannes Gutenberg prints the first Bible using movable type in Mainz, Germany.

1479

Spain is united under King Ferdinand and Queen Isabella.

1483

The Spanish Inquisition is formally established; Martin Luther is born.

1492

Christians defeat Muslims at Granada in Spain; Jews are expelled from the Spanish kingdoms; the voyage of Christopher Columbus results in the discovery of the New World.

For Further Research

Books

Peter Lewis Allen, *The Wages of Sin.* Chicago: University of Chicago Press, 2000.

Emilie Amt, *Women's Lives in Medieval Europe: A Sourcebook.* London: Routledge, 1993.

Malcolm Barber, *The Two Cities: Medieval Europe, 1050–1320.* London: Routledge, 1992.

Robert Bartlett, *Medieval Panorama.* Los Angeles: J. Paul Getty Museum, 2001.

Tania Bayard, ed., *A Medieval Home Companion.* New York: HarperCollins, 1991.

Giovanni Boccaccio, *The Decameron.* Trans. Mark Musa and Peter Bondanella. New York: New American Library, 1982.

Norman F. Cantor, *The Civilization of the Middle Ages.* Waltham, MA: Blaisdell, 1993.

———, *The Encyclopedia of the Middle Ages.* New York: Viking, 1999.

Millia Davenport, *The Book of Costume.* New York: Crown, 1948.

Geneviève D'Haucourt, *Life in the Middle Ages.* Trans. Veronica Hull and Christopher Fernau. New York: Walter, 1963.

Georges Duby, ed., *A History of Private Life: Revelations of the Medieval World.* Cambridge, MA: Belknap Press, 1988.

Carolly Erickson, *The Medieval Vision: Essays in History and Perception.* New York: Oxford University Press, 1976.

John Fines, *Who's Who in the Middle Ages.* New York: Stein and Day, 1971.

E.B. Fryde, *Peasants and Landlords in Later Medieval England.* New York: St. Martin's, 1996.

Frances and Joseph Gies, *Life in a Medieval Castle.* New York: Harper & Row, 1978.

———, *Marriage and the Family in the Middle Ages.* New York: Harper & Row, 1987.

———, *A Medieval Family.* New York: HarperPerennial, 1998.

———, *Women in the Middle Ages.* New York: Harper & Row, 1979.

Hans-Werner Goetz, *Life in the Middle Ages.* Notre Dame, IN: University of Notre Dame Press, 1993.

Douglas Gorsline, *What People Wore.* New York: Bonanza Books, 1952.

P.W. Hammond, *Food and Feast in Medieval England.* Stroud, Gloucestershire, UK: Sutton, 1993.

Sibylle Harksen, *Women in the Middle Ages.* London: Abner Schram, 1975.

Sidney Heath, *Pilgrim Life in the Middle Ages.* New York: Houghton Mifflin, 1912.

Judith Herrin, ed., *A Medieval Miscellany.* New York: Viking Studio, 1999.

George Caspar Homans, *English Villagers of the Thirteenth Century.* Cambridge, MA: Harvard University Press, 1942.

Rosemary Horrox, ed. and tran., *The Black Death.* Manchester, UK: Manchester University Press, 1994.

Cathy Jorgensen Itnyre, ed., *Medieval Family Roles.* New York: Garland, 1996.

Sherrilyn Kenyon, *Everyday Life in the Middle Ages.* Cincinnati: Writer's Digest Books, 1995.

Robert Lacey and Danny Danziger, *The Year 1000: What Life Was Like at the Turn of the First Millennium.* New York: Little, Brown, 1999.

Vicki Leon, *Uppity Women of Medieval Times.* Berkeley, CA: Conari, 1997.

Stephen Mennell, *All Manners of Food.* Oxford, UK: Basil Blackwell, 1985.

Eric Mercer, *Furniture, 700–1700.* New York: Meredith, 1969.

Ludo Milis, *Angelic Monks and Earthly Men: Monasticism and Its Meaning to Medieval Society.* Woodbridge, Suffolk, UK: Boydell, 1992.

David Nicholas, *The Growth of the Medieval City from Late Antiquity to the Early Fourteenth Century.* London: Longman, 1997.

M.M. Postan, *The Medieval Economy and Society.* Middlesex, UK: Penguin Books, 1975.

Eileen Power, *Medieval Women.* Ed. M.M. Postan. Cambridge, UK: Cambridge University Press, 1975.

Compton Reeves, *Pleasures and Pastimes in Medieval England.* Gloucestershire, UK: Allan Sutton, 1995.

Peter Rietbergen, *Europe: A Cultural History.* London: Routledge, 1998.

S.H. Rigby, *English Society in the Later Middle Ages.* New York: St. Martin's, 1995.

Marjorie Rowling, *Life in Medieval Times.* New York: G.P. Putnam's Sons, 1968.

Jeffrey L. Singman, *Daily Life in Medieval England.* Westport, CT: Greenwood Press, 1999.

R.W. Southern, *The Making of the Middle Ages.* New Haven, CT: Yale University Press, 1953.

Brian Tierney, ed., *The Middle Ages.* New York: McGraw-Hill, 1999.

Barbara Tuchman, *A Distant Mirror: The Calamitous Fourteenth Century.* New York: Knopf, 1978.

William Yenne, ed., *Dress and Decoration of the Middle Ages.* Cobb, CA: First Glance Books, 1998.

Websites

Eyewitness to History, www.ibiscom.com. This site offers eyewitness accounts of many medieval events, including the Norman Conquest (1066), the murder of Thomas Becket (1170), the Black Plague (1347), and many others.

TIMEREF.com, www.TIMEREF.com. This site offers detailed time lines for events from the years 800 through 1499 in Britain, Scotland, and Wales. Maps of castles, cathedrals, and villages are offered as well as biographies of important people during the period.

Index